create your bright ideas

READ, JOURNAL, AND COLOR YOUR WAY TO THE FUTURE YOU IMAGINE

JESS EKSTROM

ILLUSTRATED BY NADIA FISHER

An Imprint of Thomas Nelson

Create Your Bright Ideas

© 2022 Jess Ekstrom

Tommy Nelson, PO Box 141000, Nashville, TN 37214

Published in Nashville, Tennessee, by Tommy Nelson. Tommy Nelson is an imprint of Thomas Nelson. Thomas Nelson is a registered trademark of HarperCollins Christian Publishing, Inc.

Tommy Nelson titles may be purchased in bulk for educational, business, fund-raising, or sales promotional use. For information, please email SpecialMarkets@ThomasNelson.com.

ISBN 978-1-4002-3838-5 (audiobook)
ISBN 978-1-4002-3837-8 (eBook)
ISBN 978-1-4002-3836-1 (TP)

Library of Congress Cataloging-in-Publication Control Number: 2022019647

Written by Jess Ekstrom

Illustrated by Nadia Fisher

Author photograph by Viviana Garcia, Viviimage Photography

Printed in China

22 23 24 25 26 HH 6 5 4 3 2 1

Mfr: HH / Shenzhen, China / October 2022 / PO #12119538

For my grandma Joan, who taught me that if I have a
dream, then I better get on the train and chase it.

And to all the girls out there who are wondering
if it could be them, this one's for you.

Contents

Letter from Jess

Hi, _____!
(Fill in your name here.)

Jess here.

Before we get into my story, I need you to know that I'm a regular human, just like you! Sometimes you hear fancy stories about fancy people doing big, fancy things. That's not the case here. The fanciest thing about me is that sometimes I light a candle if my dog comes into the house all wet and smelly and I don't feel like cleaning. And **BOOM** that dog smell is overpowered with the lovely scent of sunshine and daffodils. But you didn't open this book for a crash course on dog smells, did you?

Let me tell you a little more about me so we can _really_ become friends.

My favorite food is tacos. (Extra guac, please!)

I love to go camping. So much so that I lived in an Airstream trailer for over two years!

I can't dance, but I do it anyway.

My favorite movie is *Toy Story*. (I love the whole franchise.)

My dog fully understands me when I talk to him.

I can spiral a football, but don't ask me to kick a soccer ball.

I once ate a dozen glazed donuts and then ran a five-mile race.

My favorite accessory is a headband. (You'll see why if you keep reading.)

And I *love* watching people chase their dreams.

I chased my big dream after I interned at the Make-A-Wish Foundation. Make-A-Wish is an incredible organization that helps kids with serious illnesses. While I worked for them, I saw a lot of kids losing their hair to chemotherapy, and these kids *loved* to wear headbands after hair loss. I did a quick Google search and realized that a lot of companies and organizations were giving these kids wigs and hats to cover their hair loss. But no one was giving headbands.

So out of my dorm room in college, I started a business called Headbands of Hope. For every headband sold, one is given to a child with an illness.

Today as I'm writing this book, we've donated over *one million* headbands to kids with illnesses all over the world. How crazy is that?

One of the things you'll learn in this book is how to be your own entrepreneur (ON-treh-preh-NYOOR). Now, if you look up the word *entrepreneur*, you might see some long and confusing definitions. So ignore all that and just know this:

To be an entrepreneur, all you have to do is live by one golden rule: create what you wish existed.

When you see a big word like *entrepreneur*, you may think you're too young or too inexperienced to be something as fancy as an *entrepreneur*. But I want you to hear something important that I figured out during my journey:

Ordinary people can do extraordinary things.

You might learn about the presidents in school or people who made history and think to yourself, *They had it all figured out! They clearly knew what they were doing. They had a plan all along to be successful.*

Allow me to let you in on a little secret:

NOBODY KNOWS WHAT THEY'RE DOING.

I want you to think of someone who is *really* successful—either a historic figure, a professional athlete, a singer, an entrepreneur, a teacher, or just someone you think did something amazing.

Write their name here: _____.

That person, no matter whose name you wrote, once had *no idea* what they were doing. Just like you and just like me.

Every expert was once a beginner.

Every single person you know who is *so successful* or *so good* at something had to start at the very beginning and learn from a blank slate.

Every basketball player once had to learn to dribble.

Every singer once had to learn do re mi.

Every architect started with LEGOs.

Every chief executive officer (CEO) started with a lemonade stand.

Every successful person started right where you're sitting, and they carried two things: the wonder of what a great future could look like and the belief that they could shape the future.

That last part is key: *belief.*

Many people want to change the world, but the ones who actually do it have something that sets them apart from the others—*the belief that they can.*

Before you continue this book, you need to promise me one thing:

Believe that it can be *you.*

YOU can be the one who people write stories about.

YOU can be the one who makes history.

YOU can be the one who solves problems.

YOU can be the one who creates necessary change.

YOU can be the one who finds the cure.

YOU can be the one who changes the world.

YOU can be the one.

When I was young, I didn't think I could be the one who starts a company that helps millions of kids. But then I did it.

So if I can do it, you can too.

That's why this book is more than just something you'll read. It's a guide to help you turn your ideas into real-life actions. Together we're going to discover your interests and

People who write down their goals are 42 percent more likely to achieve them. So start writing![1]

create a path toward doing something *extraordinary*. Here's what you can expect during our journey:

READ. First, read about how I created my bright ideas so you can learn from my wins (and my mistakes) to create your own bright ideas!

WRITE. Then it's your turn! In the "Journal Your Bright Ideas" spaces, respond to the journaling questions to get your ideas on paper.

PLAY. The "Go for It" sections will help you learn and grow. When you put the book down, try these challenges in the real world. But don't take yourself too seriously!

CREATE. Let your inner artist flourish! On these inspirational coloring pages, color and doodle your way to a brighter future. Then cut out these pages and display them in your room as a reminder of what you're capable of!

Each chapter will help prepare you for what's next in achieving your goals.

But this journey will be a whole lot easier if you start with the belief that you can do extraordinary things, just as you are.

Actually, let's get this in writing before we move on. Over the years I've discovered that contracts are *very important* in the entrepreneurship world.

> Believe that it can be *you*.

I, _____, wholeheartedly
(Print your name here.)
believe that I can do extraordinary things.

_____   _____

           Signature   Date

Phew, glad that's settled! I'll scan this and send it to my legal team, but while the ink is drying, I want you to remember this:

Ordinary people can do extraordinary things.

But let's be honest, you're *way* more than ordinary.

See you in chapter 1!

Rooting for you,
Jess

ORDINARY PEOPLE CAN DO EXTRAORDINARY THINGS.

CHAPTER ONE

Tap into Your Superpower

Have you ever said to yourself, "When I'm older, I can start on my dreams"?

I used to think that way too. I thought I had to wait until I was older, until I had more experience, until I graduated, until I felt ready. Or any other excuse I would tell myself.

But the best time to start is the moment you're inspired.

I started my business, Headbands of Hope, when I was still in school. And I'll tell you a secret that I've never told *anyone* before—I used to lie about my age. I know that lying is bad, but I thought that if people knew I was young, they wouldn't take me seriously or want to work with me.

When I got the idea to start a company that gives headbands to kids with illnesses, I second-guessed myself because I had *zero* business experience. I couldn't even spell *entrepreneur*. (Okay, I still use spellcheck for that one.) The only experience I had was selling cups of lemonade to my neighbors for seventy-five cents.

So to make up for my young age and lack of experience, I would lie about my age in hopes that people would want to work with me. I started doing this on phone calls with manufacturers, website service providers, hospital donation departments, and anyone else I needed to work with to start my business. Before I called, I would google fancy business terms like *net profit* and *minimum order quantity* and *product specs*. Then I would try to use those words in conversation to seem older and more experienced, even though I didn't know what most of the terms meant.

One day I was on the phone with the St. Baldrick's Foundation, a nonprofit organization that raises funds for childhood cancer research, and I said, "My teacher told me to start with fewer headbands first and then add more after that."

"Your *teacher*? Are you still in school?" the woman on the phone said, shocked.

I froze with the phone to my ear. I was busted.

"Yes, I'm in college at North Carolina State University," I replied.

She paused for a moment, and I held my breath.

"That's *amazing*!" she replied. "We should feature you in our newsletter and send it to our entire email list. What an incredible story: *college student starts business to give back to kids with cancer.*"

I couldn't believe it. Not only did she still want to work with me after learning my young age, but she also wanted to *highlight* it for the nonprofit's followers!

From that day forward, I started admitting my age. And let me tell you, it was the best

A *NONPROFIT* is an organization that doesn't make a profit. That doesn't mean that the people who work for the organization don't get paid. But it does mean the organization uses most of its money for a good cause. It pays all the costs related to running an organization, like rent and office supplies. Then the rest goes toward the organization's mission. Usually, if a nonprofit organization is run well, only one-fourth of its budget (or less!) is used on expenses.

decision I've ever made. Here are two great things that happened because I was a young entrepreneur:

1. I asked my teachers if I could use my business as a school project, and they all said yes! So not only did I get to use class time to work on my business, but I also got feedback from students and teachers to make my business even better.
2. I learned that there were hundreds of grants for students starting their own businesses. A grant is money given for a specific purpose that you don't have to pay back! Because of this, I received thousands of dollars that helped me build my business.

Then one day I got the most exciting email I have ever received.

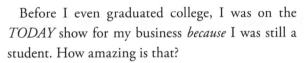

Hi, Jess!

This is Amy from NBC's *TODAY* show. We're doing a story on young entrepreneurs, and we'd love to highlight you and your business, Headbands of Hope. Can you call me at the number listed below?

Before I even graduated college, I was on the *TODAY* show for my business *because* I was still a student. How amazing is that?

Here's the moral of the story: so many great things happened for me when I started admitting my youth instead of hiding it.

So before we talk any more about how to create something *amazing*, I need you to understand this: *Your age is your superpower!* Yes, that's right.

Because you're young, you have some advantages:

1. **TIME.** You have so much time to try things, fail, and start over again. You're in the biggest "do-over" period of your life, which is *awesome* because big ideas sometimes come with big belly flops that require you to hop back on the diving board and jump again.
2. **TRENDS.** Okay, don't tell your parents I said this, but you probably know more than they do about the latest trends. You're swimming in the newest technology, TikTok dances, and ideas. A lot of times you know what the future looks like before they do. So use that to your advantage!

CHOOSE YOUR OWN TITLE

What title do you want to have someday? Do you like the idea of creating something of your own? Then you might like the title FOUNDER.

Do you prefer to take charge, solve problems, and lead others toward an important goal? Then CEO or PRESIDENT might be a good fit for you.

Do you want to spend your days skateboarding across America to raise funds for people in need? Then you might take the title CHIEF FINANCIAL SKATEBOARDER.

Imagine going after what you love to do, then use your creativity to choose a title that best fits your dreams. This is a simple way to help you decide how you might want to use your time, interests, and energy.

3. **ENERGY.** Having tons of energy is great for school, piano practice, and chores. But you can put some of that energy toward your bright ideas! Get up early before school and work on your business or big dreams, or write down your ideas while you're waiting for the bus. Or on the weekends, go to some local businesses and ask the owners about how they got started.

The more you do, the more you'll learn. And the more you learn, the better your ideas will be.

And I'll say one more thing about your age being your superpower: when you start your ideas, you're creating the future you want to live in.

Soon enough, you'll be handed the keys to this world, and you'll be deciding where to turn and where to go next.

Soon enough, you'll be the one that people look to with the title *founder, CEO, president,* or something cool like *chief happiness officer* beside your name.

Soon enough, the world's problems will be on your to-do list, and someone will ask you, "What should we do about this problem?"

Soon enough, your greatest talents will serve the world's greatest needs.

The phase that you're in now is your training period to eventually run this world. So don't think that you're too young to make an impact or that you don't have influence yet—because you actually have *more* influence on the future than anyone in a position of power right now. Why?

Because you *are* the future. What you do now changes what the world will become.

> Your greatest talents will serve the world's greatest needs.

And I am so excited to see what you create. So enough playing around. Let's get started with your ideas!

GO FOR IT

Discover what's available to you right now. Does your school have any business or sports clubs you could join, or can you start one yourself? Can you ask a teacher to give you feedback on your ideas? Do any local organizations have grants for students starting businesses? Take one step this week toward doing or creating something new.

Journal
YOUR BRIGHT IDEAS

I am _____ years old. And I am the perfect age to create my bright ideas because _____

_____.

Here are some ways I can use my time, interests, and energy to create something awesome:

_____

_____

_____

_____

_____

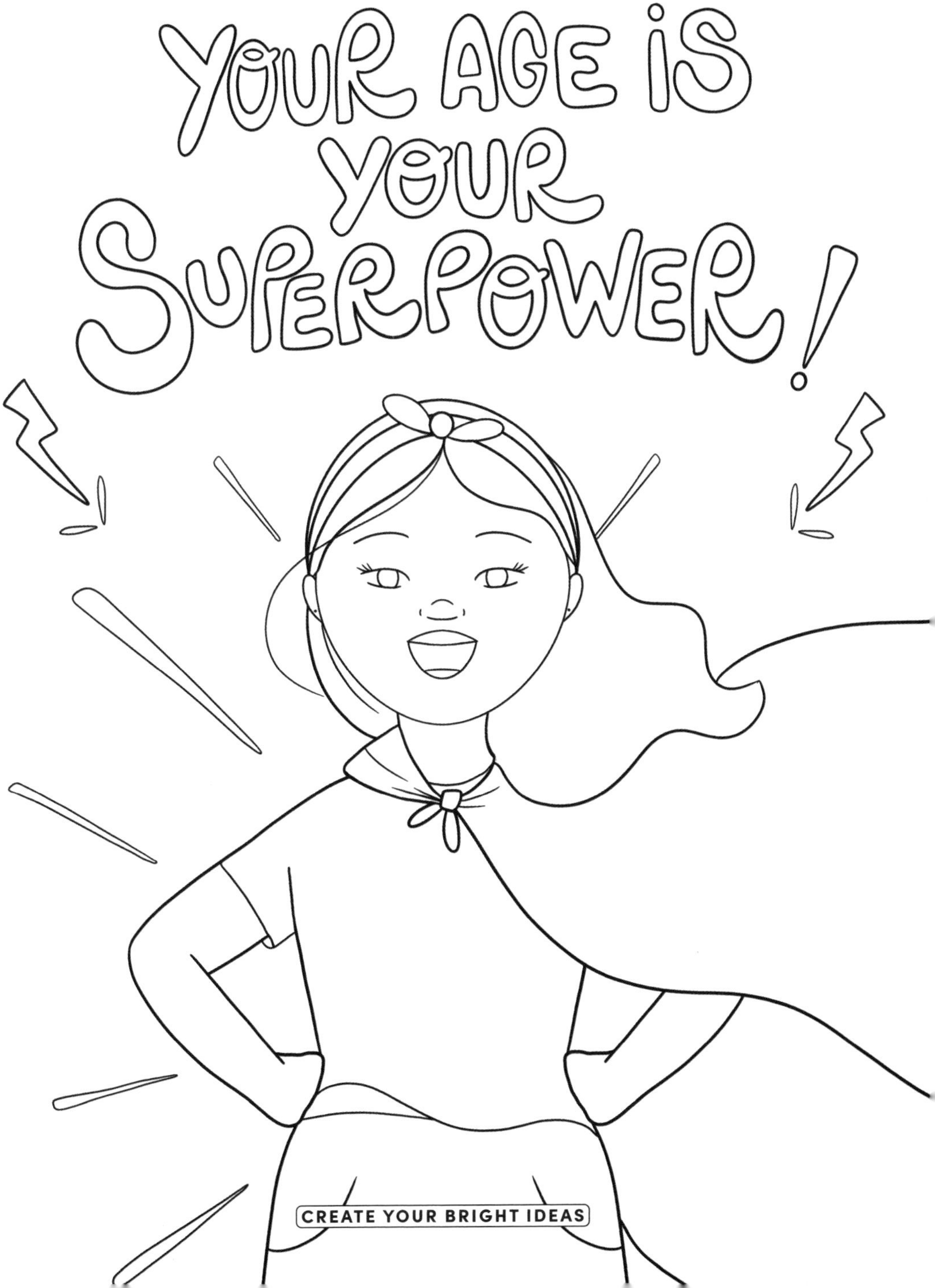
YOUR AGE IS YOUR SUPERPOWER!
CREATE YOUR BRIGHT IDEAS

CHAPTER TWO

Keep Throwing Darts

Middle school wasn't easy for me. I didn't have a lot of friends to sit with at lunch or have sleepovers with. Boys didn't ask me to dances. I got bullied about my weight and my acne. And to make matters worse, my beautifully stunning sister was one year older than me and super smart and popular. She could even do a *perfect* cartwheel. She had it all figured out.

The other kids and teachers would tell me, "Oh, you're Heather Ekstrom's sister!" But they would never call me *Jess*.

The crazy part is, sometimes when we don't get what we want, we get pushed in a new direction that can be even *better* for us.

I didn't know it at the time, but being unpopular in school was a gift because it pushed me to fill my time with something else: reading. Specifically, reading a book series called Chicken Soup for the Soul.

At lunch or during recess or on the bus, I would whip out my book and dive into that day's story. The Chicken Soup for the Soul series had different themes for each book, and each one included dozens of different stories written by people who sent their stories in.

One afternoon, while reading *Chicken Soup for the Teenage Soul*, I had a revelation: *real* people are writing these stories. I'm a real person too. So it's possible that one day I could publish a story.

And this was the moment I remember truly *wanting* something for the first time. Not wanting a snack after school. Not wanting to see the new *Toy Story* movie in theaters. Not wanting a Razor scooter.

This was a different kind of desire. I didn't want to own one more thing or be entertained by another movie. I wanted something for my life and my future. *I wanted to create.* I had a dream flash before my eyes. I imagined myself reading *Chicken Soup for the Teenage Soul* and seeing my name inside. This kind of dream was a new feeling for me.

When we discover that we want to achieve something, our mind tries to talk us out of it. So when I realized I wanted to get published in *Chicken Soup for the Teenage Soul,* my brain started saying things like this:

But you're not a writer!

You're only in sixth grade. What do you have to say?

You're not going to get this, so why even try?

What if you try and don't get published? Wouldn't you be embarrassed?

But luckily, we can figure out whether our thoughts are facts or fables.

You can sort through your thoughts and decide the negative ones are wrong.

But you're not a writer!

"Every writer had to start somewhere. Why not here?"

You're only in sixth grade. What do you have to say?

"Young people have stories too. Why not share them?"

You're not going to get this, so why even try?

"I'll try because if I don't, I'll always wonder what could have been."

What if you try and don't get published? Wouldn't you be embarrassed?

"If I try and don't get published, I'll be in the same position I'm in today. So there's only an upside to trying, not a downside to failing."

BRAIN TALK

Name one activity or goal your brain has talked you out of trying:

_____

List some of the negative thoughts that convinced you not to try it:

_____

_____

Now flip each negative thought with a positive thought:

_____

_____

Write why each positive thought is true:

_____

_____

When we respond to our negative thoughts with positive thoughts and find reasons why they're true, we realize the negative isn't so scary after all!

We talk a lot about proving ourselves to others, but most of the time, other people aren't holding us back. Our own thoughts are. Isn't that crazy?

Once I decided I would try to be published, I started writing poems and short stories every day at lunch and after school. Just call me J. K. Rowling because I was writing *a lot.*

You see, when you decide to achieve something, you get a spark of inspiration that makes you more driven than any other time in your life. That inspiration can last a day, a week, a month, or even longer.

But one thing I know is true: the longer you wait to start, the quicker that inspiration will fade.

I would write poems that were absolutely *awful.* I wrote stories that didn't even have a beginning, middle, or an end. The work I was creating was far from a masterpiece.

But with each poem or story I wrote, two important things happened:

1. **I LEARNED.** Each terrible writing submission taught me more about my own writing style. With each rejection letter I got (which was a lot), I knew the *next* story I wrote would be better.
2. **I FUELED MY INSPIRATION WITH ACTION.** Not every action I took was the *right* action, but it didn't matter. It added to my inspiration anyway. So I kept working and trying.

When we take steps toward what we want to achieve, we tell our brains, "Hey, I'm going for it! Help me get there!"

When we don't act on our ideas and instead just *think* about them, our brain will make up stories about why our ideas won't work. And we talk ourselves out of starting.

You know how in a courtroom, they show evidence to prove why someone is guilty or innocent? Like if you tell your mom you didn't have *any* cookies but there are chocolate chip crumbles all over your sweater, those crumbs are *evidence* that you're guilty as charged.

We need evidence that our ideas matter.

And when we work toward our ideas, even if the work isn't very good, it still serves as evidence that our ideas are growing.

My English teacher found out what I was doing and gave me stamps every day to mail my submissions into Chicken Soup for the Soul. I probably submitted over one hundred stories!

I received countless rejection letters that read something like, "Thank you for your submission, but we did not select your story at this time."

Our ideas matter.

Sometimes I would even use the back of the rejection letter to drum up my next submission idea. Then I'd write a new story, stick it in yet another envelope, stamp it, and send it off to the judges.

One day, I got home from school and saw a letter on the kitchen counter. It was from Chicken Soup for the Soul. But this time, it was in a different-colored envelope. It was in a yellow envelope, and it felt heavier than the rejection letters I normally got.

I ripped open the envelope, and my eyes skimmed the opening paragraph: "Congratulations! Your work has been chosen to be in *Chicken Soup for the Teenage Soul*. Enclosed is your check for seventy-five dollars for your winning submission."

I DID IT!

I spun around, stuck the letter on our refrigerator, and eagerly waited for months for the book to come out.

My mom and I walked into the Barnes & Noble in my hometown to buy it on the release date. I grabbed it off the shelf and flipped through the pages until I found my name.

And there it was: "Story by Jess Ekstrom."

That vision I had of opening this book and seeing my name was now as real as it gets. *I was holding it.*

A lot of times we think that we get what we want by having a carefully crafted plan or having loads of experience. But my journey of getting published in *Chicken Soup for the Teenage Soul* taught me that it's mainly about throwing darts.

RELENTLESS OPTIMISM is when you believe *so much* in what you're doing that you channel your go-for-it, nothing-can-stop-me attitude!

Have you ever played a game of darts? I was so bad at darts as a kid that my dad had to patch up the entire wall behind the dartboard because I missed so many times. Sorry, Dad!

But each time you throw a dart, you learn something about how to throw it. So the more darts you throw, the better your game will be and the higher the probability that you'll hit the bull's-eye.

Getting rejected over one hundred times and then finally getting a story accepted taught me a lot about success. And I realized that success can be less about having a perfect strategy and more about relentless optimism.

A perfect strategy tends to work for pilots, surgeons, and architects, but that's not the case for entrepreneurs. Entrepreneurs need relentless optimism so they'll keep trying new things—throwing dart after dart after dart—until they succeed.

WHEN YOU HAVE RELENTLESS OPTIMISM . . .

THE FAILURES STING LESS EACH TIME.

YOU BELIEVE WHOLEHEARTEDLY IN THE WORK THAT YOU'RE DOING.

YOU KEEP SHOWING UP EVERY DAY EVEN IF IT'S TO MOVE JUST ONE INCH CLOSER TO YOUR GOAL.

YOU KNOW YOUR JOURNEY WILL WORK OUT IN THE END (EVEN IF IT'S NOT WHAT YOU PICTURED).

And that's the bug I caught that day—the bug of relentless optimism. From that day forward, I cared less about what the other kids at school thought about me, and I cared more about what I thought about myself. The more I believed in my own potential, the more I would go for it, just like I did with *Chicken Soup for the Teenage Soul*.

If I could relentlessly chase this dream of getting published and make it happen, what else could I chase and achieve? What would you do differently if you believed in yourself?

GO FOR IT

Think about the last time you thought to yourself, *I'd love to do that, but I'm too nervous!* Maybe it's trying out for a sports team or asking a new friend to hang out after school. Whatever it is, just try it without worrying about the outcome. Throw the dart and see what happens!

Journal
YOUR BRIGHT IDEAS

What creative ideas and dreams are floating around in your head? Write them here:

_____

_____

_____

_____

_____

Now list ways you can throw darts and try these ideas!

_____

_____

_____

_____

_____

CHAPTER THREE

Find Inspiration from Frustration

When you think of an inventor, what comes to mind?

Do you think of someone with a lab coat and a glass container with chemicals bubbling over or someone building gadgets with wheels, testing their speed as they race down a track?

Whoever you imagine, let me ask you this:

Do you believe an inventor can be someone who is just like you?

Believe it or not, *anyone* can be an inventor or an entrepreneur. It doesn't matter your age, gender, experience, or birthplace.

All you need to do is follow one simple rule:

Create what you wish existed.

That's it. That's the membership rule. Welcome to the inventor club! You can pick up your name tag at the front desk.

I didn't understand this rule for a while. But luckily, I had a front-row seat to someone living by this rule in my own house. My dad had a pretty cool job managing health clubs and gyms. He loved it, but he had a problem: he wanted a way to remind and encourage his gym members to come back to the gym—so that they would create a routine and stick with it.

My dad looked all over for services to help him solve this problem of communicating with his gym members. And after months of searching, he came up dry.

> You don't need a fancy office to start a business. Usually, you just need your brain . . . and maybe a computer!

Have you ever looked for something that you couldn't find? Like a pair of sparkly shoes, a club to join for your favorite hobby, or a marinara sauce like your grandma makes? You search all over for it, but you can't find it. What do you feel when this happens? Frustration? I feel the same way when that happens.

But here's a trick that I want you to put in your back pocket. I call it *inspiration from frustration*.

That means whenever we feel frustration, we can also feel inspiration.

If we can't find something, maybe we can create it instead.

We think inspiration acts like a lightning bolt striking or a light bulb turning on—the clouds part, angels start singing, and we're suddenly hit with a brilliant idea. This is called an "aha moment."

But I think aha moments are extremely overrated. Most of the time, inspiration comes from something less glorious:

- Dealing with a problem we can't solve
- Having a jumbled mess in our head that we're trying to make sense of
- Seeing or experiencing injustice
- Wishing something were better or different
- Experiencing frustration

So if we're waiting for an aha moment, that's exactly what we'll end up doing. Waiting. Waiting for a good idea even though

good ideas come to us during frustrating moments. We'll be waiting for the clouds to part when an idea is born in the rain.

My dad decided to find inspiration from frustration. He told our family that he wanted to quit his job at the gym and build a technology company that reminds members to come back to the gym.

My mom hugged him and said she was proud of him.

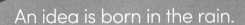

An idea is born in the rain.

My sister high-fived him and asked follow-up questions about his idea.

And I asked, "What's for dinner?"

I didn't understand why he was quitting his job to start a technology company when he could barely answer his own phone. Why would you leave a stable job to get no paycheck and pursue an idea that you're not even sure is going to work?

Over the next few months, I saw my dad renovate our upstairs bathroom and turn it into his home office. He'd be in there from the crack of dawn until dinnertime working on his business idea.

Later that year, we went on a family camping trip to Asheville, North Carolina. As my sister and my dad built the tent and my mom set up the camping chairs, I thought it would be a good idea to listen to music and be absolutely zero help. I took my headphones out of my backpack and noticed the cords were super tangled. (This was before AirPods existed.) The more I tried to untangle these cords, the more tangled they became. And the more tangled they became, the more frustrated I became.

And do you remember our golden rule? *Find inspiration from frustration.*

I turned to my dad and said, "Dad, headphone cords should just roll up like a Slinky so they never get tangled again! I'm going to *invent* that."

I stood tall like I had just solved all the world's problems with my Slinky-headphone idea.

My dad sat me down, took the headphones out of my hand, and untangled the cords in about ten seconds.

He looked at me and said, "That Slinky-headphone idea is a good one, but that's already been invented."

Shoot! There goes my billion-dollar idea, I thought.

He handed back my headphones, looked me in the eye, and said, "But I want you to keep thinking that way. Keep looking for problems, keep thinking about how the world could be better, and keep thinking about how you can fix it."

In that moment, I didn't realize the full story of how hard my dad worked on his business. His company eventually did so well that he was able to sell it to a big company. But in that moment, I learned that great business is about solving great problems.

TRY IT OUT

What's one frustration you have about your room?

_____

Now name three ideas for turning that frustration into inspiration.

1. _____

2. _____

3. _____

After my dad walked away, I just sat there with my headphone cords untangled in my hand, thinking, *Keep looking for problems. Keep thinking about how the world could be better. Keep thinking about how you can fix it.*

And just as my *Chicken Soup for the Teenage Soul* goal taught me to throw darts, this headphone moment with my dad taught me about *what* darts I wanted to throw. I wanted to throw darts that solve problems.

From that moment on, I looked at the world through a different lens. I allowed myself to believe *I could be the one* to fix problems.

And that was the moment I became an entrepreneur—when I shifted from the role of a complainer to a problem solver.

Complainers blame the world for their problems. They're quick to point out an issue and slow to react to it. Problem solvers do something about it. They don't just talk about an issue. They ask themselves, *How can I make this better?* Then they act on it.

Sometimes the answer is a quick fix, sometimes it's having the courage to stand up for someone, sometimes it's just picking up trash from the ground, and sometimes it's as big as a movement or a business idea.

Complainers wait for the solution. Problem solvers create the solution. Which one do you want to be?

GO FOR IT

The next time you feel frustrated, get excited! Instead of complaining, challenge yourself to find inspiration from that moment. Then come up with three solutions that could help fix the frustrating situation.

Journal
YOUR BRIGHT IDEAS

Make a list of your frustrations or the problems you see at school, in your community, or in the world.

What are some ideas to solve them?

CHAPTER FOUR

Take the First Step

I remember the first time I was told to run a mile. For me, a mile was basically the same distance as a flight to Europe. There was *no way* I could run a mile. But when the day came, our gym teacher shouted, "Ready, set, go!" and off we ran, four laps around the track. The first lap felt easy, the second lap my feet hurt, the third lap I was out of breath, and by the fourth lap I was sweating through my sweatshirt. (*Is that why they're called sweatshirts?!*)

Nevertheless, I miraculously crossed the finish line and plopped down on the grass. I looked down at my legs. I couldn't believe it. *These* legs ran a whole mile. What else could they do?

When I got home from school that day, I told my mom that I ran a whole mile. Maybe I should have kept that breaking news to myself because the next day she had me and my sister, Heather, sign up for an after-school program called Girls on the Run.

The very next day, at the first Girls on the Run practice, we ran a mile . . . again! This time I knew what I was in for, so I could tell myself to just keep going.

When you prove to yourself that you can do something, you have evidence of your potential. It's harder for your brain to talk you out of doing something when you know what you can achieve.

After we crossed the finish line, my sister and I felt on top of the world. We just ran a *whole* mile for the second time. Then the Girls on the Run coach told us that in just two months we would be running a 5K, also known as five kilometers. That's a whopping 3.1 miles!

That seemed *way* too long, like a lap around the world. But my sister said, "Jess, if we can run one mile, we can totally run three!"

A couple months later, we ran a 5K together. After the 5K, we ran a 10K, which is 6.2 miles. Then after the 10K, we ran a half marathon, which is 13.1 miles. After the half, my sister wanted us to run a full marathon—which is a mind-blowing, leg-killing *26.2 miles*. I told her the only way I'd do it is if we signed up for the Walt Disney World Marathon. If I'm going to run until I'm numb, I should at least do it at the most magical place on earth, right?

So we registered for the race and trained for a few months. The night before the race we did something called carb loading, where you eat carbohydrate-heavy foods—like pasta, rice, and potatoes—so your body can store energy before a big race. It was the best time of my life! (My wedding was a close second.) We went to a pasta buffet, and I felt like a baby turning one year old who gets to smash cake in their face. Alfredo, marinara, pesto, you name it—we piled it all on our plates. We came. We carbed. We conquered.

WHAT ELSE IS POSSIBLE?

What's something you've completed that you're proud of? Are you proud of teaching your dog to shake hands? Or giving a presentation to your class? Or reading an entire book series? List your achievement here:

Because you've completed that, what else is possible for you? For example, if you can teach your dog tricks, can you start teaching your neighbor's dogs tricks? List some ideas for next steps here:

The next morning, our energy was high (thank you, pasta), and we took our places behind the starting line.

At race time, the gun went off and fireworks blasted into the sky. Then I took my first step. My adrenaline was pumping, and the first three miles were a breeze. Isn't that the way most of us launch into something new and ambitious? Sure, we're nervous, but we've got a lot of energy sending us toward something exciting. But then we get thirsty, the carbs burn off, blisters form on our toes, and it isn't much fun anymore—then our energy fizzles out.

Around mile five I started to question why in the world I was

> Energy comes in waves.

doing this and asked Siri where the closest Chipotle was. I was tired. But before I mapped out my escape to Chipotle, I discovered something: energy comes in waves. I felt tired around mile five, but by mile eleven, I felt great. So for the rest of the race, whenever I was tired, I knew I would get another wave of energy soon. I would tell myself, *Hey, you're tired now. But you're going to get a boost of energy really soon. So hang on!*

Finally, we made it to the big finish-line archway. My sister and I held hands and ran through it together. *We made it!*

We found our parents at the end of the finish line and hugged, took pictures, drank lots of water, and ate lots of bagels. Then a Disney character handed us T-shirts that read, "I completed the Walt Disney World Marathon."

All those years ago, I questioned if I could run a mile, and now I had just completed over *twenty-six* miles.

My sister's running story continued. Heather eventually went on to run a **ONE-HUNDRED-MILE RACE!** But here's the thing: she would have *never* run one hundred miles if she hadn't tried to run one mile.

That first mile she ever ran was a clue to what was possible. If she could run one mile, then maybe she could run three. If she could run three, then maybe she could run ten. If she could run ten, then maybe she could eventually run one hundred.

By testing ourselves and stretching our limits, we're climbing up a ladder to discover what's possible—because we can't skip to the top of the ladder. We have to take the first step. We have to take it day by day, little by little. Because the steps you take each day will add up to something really big. One step can lead to a hundred miles.

If you're wondering what's possible for you, if you can achieve something big, remember this: the only way to find out is to try it. Either you'll discover you can do it and you can try the next challenge, or you'll learn what you need to work on before you can achieve it.

BUT THE ONLY WAY TO KNOW YOUR POTENTIAL IS BY TESTING IT.

RUN THE MILE.	**START THE BUSINESS.**
ENTER THE STUDENT COUNCIL ELECTION.	**CREATE THE CLUB.**
WRITE THE BOOK.	**VOLUNTEER AT THE SHELTER.**

When we try things that we're not sure we can do, we're training our confidence muscle. If we do only the things we already know how to do, we'll never build our confidence, we'll never get stronger, and we'll never experience the crazy-cool stuff this world has to offer. But when we're brave enough to try something without the total certainty that it will work out, we train ourselves to not just dream big but *do big*.

GO FOR IT

Remember, to run a hundred miles, you need to start by running one! Choose one thing from your "Journal Your Bright Ideas" list below and take one action toward trying out that new thing.

YOUR BRIGHT IDEAS

What are some things that you want to try but haven't yet?

_____

_____

_____

_____

_____

Now write down the next steps you have to take to try them.

_____

_____

_____

_____

_____

_____

CHAPTER FIVE

Go for It

Have you ever tried to plan out your entire life? Maybe you've even created a vision board for what you want your future to look like.

You know what career you'll have.

You know what college you'll attend.

You know what kind of house you'll live in.

You know what your hobbies will be.

You know what places you'll travel to.

You know what kind of impact you'll have on the world.

You know all of it! Because you've planned it, you've thought about it, and you've filed it away in your mind under your long list of to-dos.

But here's the truth: *you don't know any of this.*

You can have goals and dreams for your future, but you can't plan for everything, nor should you. Why? Because there are so many amazing possibilities for your life that you don't even know exist yet!

Trust me, I had my whole life planned out when I was your age. I was going to be a journalist living in Manhattan. I'd get invited to swanky parties and wear designer clothes and interview big celebrities that I'd write about for a magazine.

I had it all figured out. Or at least, I thought I did.

Then one day I was walking down a hallway during my freshman year of college, and a purple sign on a bulletin board caught my eye.

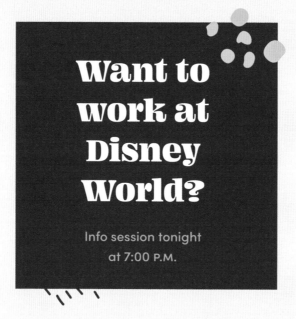

Want to work at Disney World?

Info session tonight
at 7:00 P.M.

Work at the most magical place on earth? Yes, please!

I went to the information session, and a Disney employee told us about the Disney College Program, where you work in the parks, take classes, and get college credit. It sounded like a blast, and I knew that if I applied, I could always decide later if I really wanted to go. But I wouldn't have a decision to make unless I put my name in the hat, so I did.

That night I submitted my application for the Disney College Program. Within a week or two, I had an interview call. And then a week after that, right around Thanksgiving, I received an email from the Disney Applications Office:

Miss Jess Ekstrom:

Congratulations! You've been accepted into the Disney College Program starting in January and ending in May.

Your job will be in Food & Beverage. You will get your exact location and park assignment upon arrival.

Please let us know within 48 hours if you'll be coming to Orlando in January. We hope to have you!

Sincerely,
The Disney College Program

I couldn't believe it. There were so many thoughts and questions running through my mind:

I got accepted! Woohoo!

I'll be working in Food & Beverage. Does this mean I get to eat the food too?

What is my favorite Disney movie? I need to be ready to answer these kinds of questions!

Holy guacamole, I have only two days to decide if I'm doing this. And if I do it, I'll leave in one month for an entire semester!

How was I going to make this decision so quickly? I racked my brain with all the things I'd need to do.

I'd need to cancel my classes for the next semester. I'd need to tell my roommate she'd need to find a replacement. I'd need to find housing in Orlando.

Ah! Too many things!

But when you really want to do something, all those messy details find a way of working themselves out.

However, I still didn't know if the Disney College Program was something I *really* wanted to do.

How do you know when you should go for it?

Well, I'm about to show you!

At that moment, while facing a big decision, I created a habit that has

Go FoR It!

helped me make thousands of decisions.

I created a "Worst and Best List."

Here's how it works: First you list the *worst* things that could happen if you decide to go for it. Then you list the *best* things that could happen if you decide to go for it. And then you decide if any of the *best* things are better than the possibility of any of the *worst* things!

You may have heard of a "Pros and Cons List." That's where you write the positives and negatives of an opportunity in that moment. But the "Worst and Best List" is about dreaming of outcomes for the future. What are the worst and best things that could happen?

Sometimes, when you write out the worst things that could happen and see it on paper, you realize they aren't that bad after all. And the chance for reaching the *best* things may feel greater than the chance of the worst things happening.

So for the Disney College Program, my list looked like this:

The Worst

1. What if I make zero friends? I'm going by myself!
2. What if I hate my job?

3. What if I'm not good at it?
4. What if I fall behind in school?
5. What if my college credits don't transfer?
6. What if my friends at school move on without me?

The Best

1. I could *love* it there.
2. I could learn a lot about business working for Disney.
3. My friends and family could visit, and I could take them to all the parks and give them FastPasses so they could skip the lines!
4. I could meet new friends from all over the world.
5. I could learn new skills.
6. I could have Disney on my résumé and get great future job opportunities.
7. I could go on a date with Prince Charming!

Okay, the last one is a bit of a stretch, but you get my point.

Once you write down "The Worst" and "The Best," your mind is free! You don't have to figure out the answer with all those thoughts floating around. You can just look at your piece of paper and make decisions.

Now it's your turn to try it!

What's a big goal or dream that you have? Write it here:

Now, imagine going for that goal. What's the worst and the best things that could happen?

The Worst

1.
2.
3.
4.
5.
6.

The Best

1.
2.
3.
4.
5.
6.

Now, looking at these lists you've written, what do they tell you? Maybe "The Worst" is not as bad as you thought it would be. And if any of those things do happen, figure out how you could handle it so that you'll feel prepared.

But now let's focus on "The Best." What if just *one* of those things happened. Would it be worth it to you? What if two, three, or even four of those things happened? Would it be worth it to go for it?

I hope you're nodding your head **YES**! And you know what? There are even more of "The Best" things that are possible for you, but you just can't see them yet. If you stick so closely to your plans and vision board that you don't open your life to other possibilities, you could miss out on the very best opportunities that cross your path!

Okay, so back to my list. I decided that the possibility of "The Best" outweighed "The Worst," so I emailed them back: **I'M IN!**

A few weeks later, I shoved six months' worth of clothes into a suit-case, waved goodbye to my family, and headed south to Orlando.

When I drove under the Walt Disney World arched sign, I got goose bumps on my arms and butterflies in my stomach. *What did I just get myself into?* I thought to myself.

The truth is, I had no idea what I had gotten myself into.

Because little did I know at the time, that decision to say yes and choose to believe in "The Best," was about to change *everything* for me.

GO FOR IT

Next time you're faced with an opportunity, even if it feels small, like joining an after-school club or volunteering at a park on a Saturday, try the "Worst and Best List" list method—and see where it takes you!

Journal
YOUR BRIGHT IDEAS

Imagine your best self in ten years. Who are you? What do you do? Where do you live? Journal or doodle it here!

What amazing possibilities could happen in your life? You could become a world-famous chef with restaurants in all the big cities. You could invent a chip that allows your dog to talk to you. You could build hundreds of schools in places that need them. Don't limit yourself. Just dream! Write down everything that's possible for you—the crazier the better.

And **THIS** is just scratching the surface!

CHAPTER SIX

Make Magical Moments

For the first few months, my job at Disney World was scooping ice cream in the Magic Kingdom on Main Street. My right bicep got super strong from scooping all day, but I'd also eat Mickey Mouse sundaes during my shifts, so it was a good balance.

At Disney World I got to meet students from all over the world who were also in the college program. I got to learn about business from one of the biggest companies in the world. But the thing I loved most was something Disney called "making magical moments."

A MAGICAL MOMENT: when a cast member (Disney refers to their employees as "cast members") does something kind and make someone's day for no reason at all.

You could surprise a random guest with FastPasses to the new Toy Story Mania! ride.

You could upgrade someone's single-scoop ice cream to a massive sundae with sprinkles and fudge.

You could give a little kid some Mickey Mouse ears as they walked into the park for the first time.

Or you could delight a couple on their

honeymoon with a chance to be a part of the *Beauty and the Beast: Live on Stage* show.

Disney is where I learned that small magical moments can make a big impact.

To help other people, you don't have to raise a ton of money or build a house or know everything about how the world works. You can help in small, unexpected ways.

I loved working at Disney so much that I decided to extend my six-month internship and stay over the summer. That meant Disney would put me in a different role, so I wouldn't be scooping ice cream anymore. I had no idea what role I would get, but I was willing to take my chances. Then one day, I got an email:

> Miss Jess Ekstrom:
>
> Your new role will be a PhotoPass photographer in Hollywood Studios. Please see the attached schedule for your photography training days.
>
> Sincerely,
> The Disney Casting Department

I couldn't believe it! Me? A *photographer*? I could barely get my head in the frame when I took a selfie. But I guess that didn't matter to them. They were going to teach me!

Sometimes we think that to do or be something, we need to have done it before. But that can't be true, because everyone who is really good at something once had to do it for the first time! I had no idea how to be a photographer, but I was about to learn.

Next time you get the chance to do something you've never done before, don't pressure yourself to be an expert in a beginner's arena. Think of it like being a kid in a sandbox, where you learn by doing, not by watching.

I showed up to my first day of training wearing my PhotoPass photographer costume that Disney provided for me. It included blue shorts, a white shirt, and a vest. Then they gave me a badge that read "Earning my ears!" to show that I was in training.

I learned about the photo settings on the camera, how to position people for a good photo, how to shoot with a tripod in night mode, and how to develop the film so the guests could purchase their pictures in the park. Finally, I was ready to shoot.

One day I was snapping photos of people who wanted their picture taken in front of the Tower of Terror. One family had a beautiful child with red hair and a badge on her shirt that read "Make-A-Wish." As I said before, the Make-A-Wish Foundation is an incredible organization that grants wishes to kids with serious illnesses. This girl's wish was to go to Disney World.

You learn by doing.

I posed this girl and her family in silly ways, including screaming on the Tower of Terror or holding Tinker Bell in their hands (that I later added using Photoshop). The family thanked me and said they couldn't wait to see their pictures when they got home.

As I watched them walk down Sunset Boulevard, while still holding my camera, I had this warm feeling inside of me.

For the first time, I knew what it felt like to be a small part of something bigger than myself. I loved being able to take photos for that family on their Make-A-Wish trip, and I wanted to chase that feeling.

I wanted to make more magical moments for families who needed them.

When I got home from work, I put some popcorn in the microwave and rushed over to my computer. I opened a Google tab and typed *volunteer opportunities at Make-A-Wish*.

As I scrolled through the photos of all the amazing wishes, my excitement grew bigger than the popcorn bag in the microwave. I found a contact form on the website and knew this was my chance to put my name in the hat.

I was ready to make more magical moments.

WHEN YOU START SOMETHING NEW

If you're a beginner, you can't expect to be perfect. But you can expect some things:

- You'll mess up—a lot. And that's normal!
- You'll learn from other people who have done it before.
- You'll have to try, try, and try again until you get it right.
- You won't be someone's first pick when they need something done quickly, and that's okay! You'll get there soon enough.
- You'll find that learning is the only way to no longer be a beginner.

Treat new things like being in a sandbox. Try, build, play, and try again.

I didn't know it at the time, but thinking about how to create magical moments for others trained me to be an entrepreneur. To create a magical moment, you have to observe the world around you and look for opportunities that can bring joy, ease, and excitement to someone who needs or deserves it.

Anytime you can identify a need, problem, or desire, you can create a magical moment for someone else.

And behind every magical moment is a business idea to keep the magic going time and time again. When you create a business, you're developing a system where magical moments can continue to be served every time you have a customer.

Starting a business is really about creating magical moments for others. If you can get into the habit of finding opportunities to create magical moments, not only will you make people's lives better and spread joy, but you'll also be training yourself to be an entrepreneur.

GO FOR IT

Create five magical moments for others this week. Write down what they were, how the person responded, and how you felt afterward.

Journal
YOUR BRIGHT IDEAS

Have you ever had a magical moment happen for you? What was it, and how did it make you feel?

How can your dreams provide magical moments for others?

MAKE MAGICAL MOMENTS.

CREATE YOUR BRIGHT IDEAS

CHAPTER SEVEN

Shoot Your Shot

The perfect moment to start pursuing your dream is when you feel the first spark of inspiration. Inspiration pumps gasoline into your energy tank. Then your progress makes you more and more excited about your dreams, and that pours even more gasoline into your energy tank.

But when we sit on an idea and don't do anything about it, that energy begins to fade.

When I got home from my Disney World internship, I felt like anything was possible. And I was excited about the idea of emailing the Make-A-Wish Foundation to see if I could intern for them the following summer. I knew I shouldn't put off sending the email because my courage and inspiration might fade away, so I quickly typed up an email that I hoped would get their attention.

Here is what it said:

Hi!

My name is Jess Ekstrom. I recently interned at Disney World as a PhotoPass photographer, and I loved photographing families who were on their Make-A-Wish trip.

I would love to intern at your Charlotte office this summer! I'm studying communications at North Carolina State University, but I can help in any area that you need.

Thank you for your consideration, and I look forward to hearing from you!

Sincerely,
Jess Ekstrom

After that I waited . . . and waited . . . and waited some more. Until a month later, an email popped up in my inbox from Make-A-Wish.

Dear Miss Ekstrom,

Thank you so much for your interest in working with our organization! At this time, we don't have an internship program in place. So please apply again next year when we do!

All the best,
Make-A-Wish

I sat there staring at the email and reread it ten times. I was about to close my computer and call it a day when I had an idea.

If they don't have an internship program in place yet, maybe I could help them build it!

If there's something you really want, make it easier for people to say yes to you by doing the work for them. Since they didn't have an internship program set up yet, having someone (hopefully me!) help them create it would be valuable to them.

So I decided to shoot my shot. I hit reply and typed this:

Thank you for getting back to me! I really want to be a part of your organization next summer, so I have an idea.

What if I help get an internship program in place? I could draw from my experience interning at Disney World. And then I can help with any tasks that people don't want to do: taking out the trash, making coffee, organizing cabinets, you name it!

Let me know your thoughts!

Sincerely,
Jess Ekstrom

To my surprise, they loved the idea, and a few months later, I was starting my summer internship.

I want to pause here for a second because this is an important part of the story. If I hadn't tried again after they said no to me, the rest of my story would not have happened.

Oftentimes, we're taught *not* to be persistent so that we don't seem obnoxious or pushy. But if you truly believe you can help, don't be afraid to ask, "Are you open to another idea?" or "Can you give me feedback so I can improve?" Shoot your shot! It's important to respect the boundaries, advice, and rules of parents and teachers, but you can also respectfully share new ideas that better fit their needs after you understand them.

I know someone who landed a dream job after he was denied for it. After he received a rejection letter, he asked the company for feedback on why he didn't get the job. It turns out, it was a test. The company rejected *all* their

> Don't be afraid to try again.

top applicants just to see who would come back and fight for it. He was the only one who did, so he got the job! How crazy is that?

If there's something you want and you're told no, ask for feedback so you can improve. And if you can work through any of the reasons they give you (like if the company doesn't have an internship program yet), let them know. You never know what could happen!

TRY IT OUT

If your coach doesn't put you in the game, ask what you need to do and improve on to earn a spot in the next game.

If you get an answer wrong on a quiz that you believe could be right, share your reasoning for your answer with your teacher. Either they'll see your reasoning and give you points for it, or they'll instruct you so you can better understand the right answer!

If you try to understand someone instead of complaining to them, then you can respect their boundaries while still improving your work.

You won't get everything you want in life. In fact, *most of the time* you won't get what you want. I still get told no all the time! But every *no* means you're reaching for something, which is a good thing. If you're only asking questions you know will get a *yes*, then you're playing it too safe.

The *nos* are proof that you're going for it.

So ask for feedback, then come back with new ideas. Either you'll learn how to improve, or you'll win them over. Either way, it's a great outcome.

But this part of my story was official: I was going to be a summer intern for Make-A-Wish.

GO FOR IT

Next time you hear a no, ask if they're open to trying a new solution or giving you feedback on how to improve. Afterward, record what you said and how they responded!

Journal
YOUR BRIGHT IDEAS

Think about your big dreams for your life. What step toward your dream have you not started on yet because you're afraid of rejection?

_____

_____

_____

_____

_____

If you are rejected, how will you respond?

_____

_____

_____

_____

_____

BEHIND EVERY BIG YES IS A PILE OF SMALL NOS.

CREATE YOUR BRIGHT IDEAS

CHAPTER EIGHT

Make It Matter

On the first day of my Make-A-Wish Foundation internship, I walked into the office with butterflies in my stomach and too much caffeine in my blood.

Will they like me? What if I make a mistake? What if I don't know what I'm doing?

When it's your first day or first time trying something new, it's natural to feel jittery while a million doubts swirl around in your head. When we don't know what the future holds, our minds try to fill in the blanks with what could go wrong.

But instead of thinking of the worst possible outcomes, ask yourself, *What could go right?*

We spend so much time focusing on doubts when we could be focusing on wonderful possibilities.

Remember, you're not going to be an expert at anything on your first try.

Everyone once had to learn how to walk.

> How long does it take to become pretty good at a new skill? Only twenty hours! That's about forty-five minutes a day for a month.[1]

Every chef once had to learn how to crack an egg.

Every Olympic ice skater once had to learn how to balance on skates.

Every mathematician once had to learn $1 + 1 = 2$.

What is something that is easy for you to do now, but you once had to learn how to do it?

See, if you can learn to do whatever *that* is, then you can learn to do anything. And if everyone had to start somewhere, why not here? And if anyone could do what it takes to become good at it, then why not you?

Every expert was once a beginner, so don't be too hard on yourself on your first day pursuing a new dream or creating a new idea. Give yourself some time to learn the ropes because you are *just* getting started.

My first day on the job at Make-A-Wish was a whirlwind. I did everything from making coffee, to organizing supply closets, to cold-calling people over the phone for donations, to licking envelopes for the gala invitations, to filing paperwork. My favorite thing was when we'd receive thank-you cards from the families, with photos of their wish experience.

One kid wanted to learn how to play basketball, and we brought in *the* Michael Jordan to teach him how to play!

Another kid wanted to ride a tractor, so we took him to the John Deere Tractor & Engine Museum to ride all their tractors.

My favorite wish was made by a girl who wanted to be a judge on a cooking show, so she got to try all the amazing foods. Yum!

I realized that no matter how small my tasks were, they were all a part of making these wishes come

> If everyone had to start somewhere, why not here?

true. Every single thing I did—whether I was taking out the trash or licking an envelope—was a part of the bigger story of making kids' wishes come true.

Have you ever been a part of something that you believed in? What was the mission?

How did it feel to work on something you believed in?

What tasks did you do, and how can you connect those tasks to the greater mission?

Sometimes when we want to make a big impact, we imagine ourselves doing the *big* thing. But doing the small stuff is just as impactful because the small things *make* the big things possible. Don't fall for the lie that to make an impact you must be front and center of the show, for all to see. You can make a great impact behind the scenes.

When you know that every task you're a part of, no matter how big or small, is a part of a bigger mission you believe in, then your work will help you feel fulfilled. A job isn't just about getting a paycheck. It can be about this deep sense of peace, knowing that your effort is building something greater than you.

Fulfillment comes from knowing that one day you can look back at your work and say things like this:

"Wow, I was a part of building something really wonderful."

"My work mattered."

"I left the world a little bit better than how I found it."

"I helped a lot of people."

I wish there was a quiz you could take that told you *exactly* what your purpose is. But the only way to figure it out is by trying new things, solving new problems, and paying attention to when you feel most excited and passionate. When something you enjoy overlaps with something that helps others, then you've found something you should pursue!

During my summer at Make-A-Wish, I knew all my small tasks were a part of making wishes come true for kids with life-threatening illnesses. Because of that experience, something inside my brain shifted. My goals for my life changed. No longer did I care about having a fancy journalist job in Manhattan and going to swanky parties. (That was my dream!) I wanted to do something that mattered. I wanted to jump out of bed every day, knowing that my day was going to count toward something bigger.

When I had just a few weeks left of my internship, my boss called me into her office.

"Jess, you've done a great job this summer, and we're really grateful for all of your help. For your last few weeks, we would like to give you a little bit more responsibility," she said with a grin on her face.

"Oh, yeah?" My ears perked up. "What did you have in mind?"

My boss slid a folder toward me across her desk. I opened it up and saw an adorable picture of a little girl alongside her entire "wish" profile.

NAME: Renee
AGE: 4 years old
ILLNESS: Brain cancer
WISH: To go to Disney World. She wants to meet Sleeping Beauty.

"You are going to help us make this wish come true. We want you to be the wish coordinator for Renee."

"Are you serious?" I shouted a little too loudly. I had never coordinated a wish before, and I was so excited to get this responsibility.

"Very serious," she replied. "But this wish needs to happen soon, her family says. She hasn't been doing well lately."

"Got it. I won't let you down!" I ran out of her office and started to plan Renee's trip to Disney World to meet Sleeping Beauty.

GO FOR IT

This week, try something you've never done before. When doubt creeps in and your brain tells you all the things that *could* go wrong, ask yourself, "What could go right?"

65

YOUR BRIGHT IDEAS

What's a big thing you want to do?

_____

_____

_____

_____

_____

What are all the little things that make that big thing possible?

_____

_____

_____

_____

_____

_____

CHAPTER NINE

Choose the Better Story

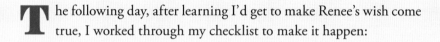

T he following day, after learning I'd get to make Renee's wish come true, I worked through my checklist to make it happen:

☐ Call Disney Parks and make sure Sleeping Beauty will be available to greet Renee and her family and attend each meal with them.

☐ Make Renee an appointment at the Bibbidi Bobbidi Boutique so she can get a Sleeping Beauty makeover.

☐ Plan a princess-themed party with Renee and all her friends.

☐ Book travel and accommodations for the family.

I finished my list and was about to coordinate more character meet and greets when my boss called me back into her office. I walked in with my notepad, ready to take on any additional tasks needed for this wish. But when I stepped into her office, I could tell by the somber look on her face that something was wrong.

"Everything okay?" I asked, tucking my pen behind my ear.

"Not really," she said. She inhaled deeply. "Renee was rushed to the hospital last night. She's not doing well, and the doctor said she can't travel. We're going to have to cancel her trip to Orlando next week."

As the words sank in, I felt a pang in my chest. And I knew my pain and disappointment were a fraction of what Renee must have been feeling in that moment. All she wanted was to meet Sleeping Beauty.

I kept thinking, *This can't be the end of the story.*

We all have experiences that we can't control. We can't control what the weather is outside. We can't control how the other kids at school treat us. And we can't control if our bus arrives late.

But our *story* is something we have more control over than you may think. Our story consists of two things:

1. How we interpret our past
2. How we choose to act in the future

You can't always control what happens in your life (your experiences), but you can control the meaning you give to an experience and what you do next (your story).

You can always choose the better story.

You see, your *experience* might be that you didn't make your school's volleyball team. But your *story* could be that you used the time you would have spent playing volleyball to instead start your own after-school nature-walking club.

You didn't get to decide if you were on the team, but you get to decide what happens next in your story.

I couldn't cure Renee's illness. I couldn't wave a magic wand and make her well enough to travel to Disney World. But maybe I could change the story.

I looked down at her folder. I knew I couldn't send her to Disney World, but maybe I could still make part of her wish come true.

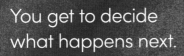

You get to decide
what happens next.

I ran back to my computer and googled *costume shops near me.*

I picked up the phone and called each costume shop to see if a Sleeping Beauty costume was available. When I finally found one, I told them the costume was for a special wish made through the Make-A-Wish Foundation and I needed it that day. They graciously donated the costume to us, and I hopped in my car to go pick it up.

When I got back to the office, I went into the bathroom, pulled up a picture of Sleeping Beauty on my phone, and did my best to transform myself into her. I tied my hair in a short bun and pulled the long blonde wig and tiara over my head. Then I stepped into the puffy pink dress and silver slippers.

I headed downstairs to find that my boss had rented a limo for our surprise mission. As I walked toward the limo using my best Disney princess walk, my boss and some of the other members of the Make-A-Wish team clapped and bowed at my grand entrance.

"Your Majesty, your chariot awaits," said the driver, who opened my door.

When we arrived at Renee's house, her mom and dad were standing outside to greet us, and they couldn't contain their excitement.

"Sleeping Beauty!" Renee's mom exclaimed. "Oh my goodness, Renee is going to be *so thrilled* that you're here. She reads your book every night and watches the movie every weekend."

"Just so you know," she added, "Renee has been very tired, and she doesn't have her eyes open right now. We believe she can hear us, but she will likely keep her eyes closed."

"That's perfectly fine," I said. "Let's go meet her!"

CHoose tHe
BetteR StoRy.

"Renee, you have a visitor!" her mom exclaimed as we walked into the house.

"Hello, Princess Renee," I said. "My name is Aurora, but some people call me Sleeping Beauty. I brought you a dress and a crown from my kingdom." I laid them on top of her bed. "I'm going to sit by your bed and read you my story. I hear it's one of your favorites!"

I sat down in a chair next to Renee's bed and started reading the story of *Sleeping Beauty* page by page.

"And they lived happily ever after. The end." I closed the book and turned to Renee. Her eyes started to flutter open, and for a brief moment, she looked at me.

We locked eyes, and I smiled at her and whispered, "Princess Renee, it's me, Sleeping Beauty."

She held my gaze for a moment, then closed her eyes again. I looked up at her mom and dad, who were in tears. "She saw you," her mom said. "She opened her eyes and saw you. Her wish has come true."

After spending a few hours at their house in character, it was time to go. I blew Renee a kiss and said she was welcome at my castle any time. I curtsied to her parents, walked down their front steps, and got back into the limo. Once I shut the door, a tidal wave of emotions crashed over me. I was trying so hard to keep it together for Renee, and when my boss dropped me off at my own car, I went inside, shut the door, and began to cry.

As I was driving home, I started to think, *Where do I put this pain? What's my story? Where do I go from here?*

Everything I thought I knew about myself changed. It was as though any plans I had for my future dissolved in front of my eyes, and I was now staring at a blank canvas. What if my future would be entirely different from what I had imagined? What if my future would be devoted to doing something good for the world? I knew that with my original plan to be a journalist, I could still do great things for others, but I wanted to build something of my own.

Sometimes we want to believe that the start of good things comes from an aha moment or a really happy moment. But sometimes, great movements, ideas, progress, and change begin during the hard times.

Because hard times give us a choice:

They can be the *excuse* for doing LESS, or they can be the *reason* for doing MORE.

MY EXCUSE

When I was in middle school, I really wanted to be on the student council. I ran for office, but I didn't win. After that, I used that disappointment as an excuse not to do anything else because I was embarrassed about losing. I stopped signing up to volunteer, and I didn't raise my hand to help out when I could have. I realize now that I could have done some fun and helpful things with or without the student council title!

You see, you don't have to hide behind the things that don't work out. I learned that the hard way. Instead, find ways to move past it and work hard at doing the things you really want to do!

Don't wait for the good times to think about what your story is or where you belong. Inspiration is born during difficult circumstances. If everything is good, why change? If everything is perfectly fine where you are—the sun is shining, the birds are chirping, and you don't have a care in the world—then you don't need to change a thing! But when you experience something tough, the wheels in your head start turning because you want to make it better.

One of my favorite analogies is this: boiling water can soften a potato but harden an egg. I'm sure you're thinking, *That's a cool fact, Jess. But why are you giving me a cooking lesson right now?*

I'll tell you why: because the exact same environment (boiling water) can provide two completely different outcomes (hard or soft).

That means the outcome is not decided by what's happening around us but by who we are becoming. You can't control the temperature of the water, but you can control how it affects you.

One single experience can write two completely different stories.

Maybe your math teacher asked you to stay after class to help you learn something you got wrong. You could tell yourself, "I'm not good at math!" Or you could say, "Lucky me, I'm going to use this time with my teacher to become the best math student in class!"

How you respond determines what happens next in your life. If you can create a better story, then you'll find that your big dreams, your business plan, and your world-changing ideas aren't out of reach.

Back at the Make-A-Wish offices, a lot of the kids we worked with experienced hair loss as a side effect of chemotherapy. I saw from photos that the staff would offer them wigs and hats, which they sometimes liked to wear. But other times, the kids didn't want to wear something that covered up their head and hid their experience. They just wanted to feel good about themselves in their own skin!

To do that, I'd see them wear colorful headbands and bandanas.

Headbands allowed them to add a fun accessory to their outfit without covering up their heads. I also love headbands, so I always enjoyed seeing kids wearing them.

Then I had a thought.

Maybe I could find a way to give headbands to kids with illnesses.

I knew I didn't want my time with Renee to be the *excuse* for why I did less. I wanted it to be the *reason* for why I did more. I wanted to be able to look back, years from now, and say "Because of Renee, I did _____."

And though I didn't know it at that time, what I created next was going to help millions of people.

GO FOR IT

When you talk about your day to your parents or friends, focus on telling the *good* story. You can't control what happens in your life, but you can always write the story of what happens next. So practice telling a good one!

Journal
YOUR BRIGHT IDEAS

Write about a tough experience you've had.

Write what your *excuse* to do less could be:

Now write the *reason* you could do more:

CHAPTER TEN

Don't Wait for the Aha Moment

After my internship at the Make-A-Wish Foundation, I went back to college for the fall semester. One day we had a guest speaker who I was so pumped to hear from. His name was Blake Mycoskie, and he was the founder of a footwear company called TOMS. For every pair of shoes sold, they donated a pair to a child in need. He called this the "One for One" model.

As I listened to him speak, the wheels in my heard started turning.

What if I could create a similar business with headbands? During my experience with Renee, I saw how impactful a small headband accessory could be for kids with illnesses. What if I started a company, and for every headband I sold, I could donate a headband to a child with an illness?

This "What if . . ." idea was a defining moment for me.

I got back to my dorm (after I asked Blake to sign my pair of TOMS shoes!), pulled out a sheet of paper, and wrote this:

SELL A HEADBAND → GIVE A HEADBAND
TO KIDS WITH ILLNESSES

Usually in cartoons and movies, when someone has an idea, a massive whiteboard appears out of the sky, and they start writing and writing, the idea growing bigger and bigger. But whiteboards don't appear out of the sky. Ideas start as a single spark, and *then* you decide if you're going to turn that spark into a flame.

In fact, I would say having a "What if . . ." idea is like discovering a balloon. Deflated, it's just a piece of flimsy rubber. But it could become a big, beautiful balloon full of air, soaring above you. You have to decide which one your idea is going to be.

For your "What if . . ." idea to be like a balloon that grows, you have to breathe life into it. You have to stop what you're doing, pick it up, take a deep breath, and put effort into it.

Our "What if . . ." ideas can be fleeting thoughts that we forget years from now, or they can be the most defining moments in our lives. You choose if your idea is just a piece of flimsy rubber or a big, beautiful soaring balloon.

Would you rather be the person who says, "I created seat belts for dogs," or the person who says, "Ugh! Seat belts for dogs was *my* idea!"

I'm guessing you picked the

CREATE YOUR BRIGHT IDEAS

Make a list of your "What if . . ." ideas. Don't think—just finish this sentence with whatever comes to mind first.

WHAT IF _____

WHAT IF _____

WHAT IF _____

WHAT IF _____

WHAT IF _____

first option. And how cool would it be to drop that line at parties or on your business card?

Jess Ekstrom, Creator of Seat Belts for Dogs
Your dog's safety is *my* priority.

We can paint sparkles around the word *inspiration* all we want, but inspiration itself is just a deflated rubber balloon. *Action* is what leads to a soaring balloon that we all love and hear stories about.

I wonder what it was like to be the person who invented the

stethoscope and heard a person's heartbeat clearly for the first time or what it was like to be the person at Netflix who created the "Skip Intro" button. And I can't help but wonder what that moment was like when the first light bulb flicked on. Those moments occurred a long time after someone had a "What if . . ." idea. And they chose whether to leave that idea lifeless, like a deflated balloon, or to give that idea life by taking action.

STARTING TIME

The best day to start is on a day that ends in *y*. Fill out the calendar with your plans to get started on your dreams.

Sunday	
Monday	
Tuesday	
Wednesday	
Thursday	
Friday	
Saturday	

Maybe you turn your idea into a club at your school.

Or maybe you create a social media account for your idea.

Or maybe you sell the products you make at your local farmer's market.

Or maybe you walk into your favorite store and ask if *they* will sell your product in their store.

Or maybe you ask for help creating a website for your business idea.

You could be the one to make something better.

Don't wait for the aha moment. Instead, listen for your own "What if . . ." ideas when you realize something could be better. And **YOU** could be the one to make it better!

I looked back down at my notebook and wrote this: *Headbands of Hope. For every headband sold, we donate one to a child with an illness.*

Below that, I wrote this: *Step 1.*

I didn't know what step one was yet, but I knew I was going to start tomorrow.

GO FOR IT

Choose one of your "What if . . ." ideas you wrote on page 81 in the "Create Your Bright Ideas" section. This week, take one small action toward that idea!

Journal
YOUR BRIGHT IDEAS

Write down any dream, business plan, or world-changing idea you have. How does it help people? How can it make the world better? By answering these questions, you're discovering the purpose behind your ideas!

CREATE YOUR BRIGHT IDEAS

CHAPTER ELEVEN

Figure It Out

Have you ever said these things to yourself?

I want to _____ , but I don't know how!

I want to _____ , but I don't know where to begin!

I want to _____ , but I've never done it before!

This is exactly what I was feeling when I got the idea for Headbands of Hope. I knew I wanted to start a business that gives headbands to kids with illnesses, but how would I even do that? Where would I begin? How would I get the headbands made? How much would I charge for each headband? How would I build a website?

The list of things I had to learn how to do was never-ending. Now that I think about it, starting a business was just one giant list of things I had never done before. My to-do list might as well have included taming a lion, finding a pot of gold, creating a juggling dance routine, and learning to speak French. That's how hard it all seemed at the beginning.

But here's the thing: *everyone* who has done something great had to learn how to do it for the first time. They *had* to move past the fear of the unknown and tackle one to-do list item at a time. After all, it's impossible to start something new without learning new things.

Entrepreneurship is not a special thing reserved for the experts. In fact, the only thing you need to become an entrepreneur is the confidence that you will take the next step. You don't need to know what you're doing. You just need to know that you can figure it out. You don't need to start with all the bells and whistles. You just need to start.

E-COMMERCE means buying and selling products online.

I sat on my bed in my dorm room, looking at my notebook with *Headbands of Hope* scribbled at the top. I needed a place to start, so I wrote a to-do list of all the things I would have to figure out how to do. I call this list the Unstoppable Action Plan.

On the left side of the paper, I wrote all the things I needed to do that seemed easy. On the right side, I wrote all the things that made me think, *Whoa, how in the world do I do* that?

Jess's Unstoppable Action Plan

Easy Things

1. Create a name for the business.
2. Draw a logo.
3. Make a website, then tell my friends and family about my idea to get feedback and support.

Hard Things

1. Find a manufacturer to create the headbands. (I can't sew!)
2. Register my business in the state I live.
3. Price my product.
4. Figure out how shipping works.

When you start with the easy things first, a few things happen:

- You **START** because you're not paralyzed by figuring out the hard things.
- You cross things off your list. (Go you!)
- By doing the easy things, you learn more about how to do the hard things. And then the hard things don't seem so scary.

That's what happened when I made my list. First, I went to the website GoDaddy.com and purchased the domain HeadbandsofHope.com. Woohoo! Step one, complete. (Do a happy dance!)

Then I needed to create a logo. I didn't know anything about graphic design, but I had a friend who was in a graphic design class. So one day, I introduced myself to her teacher. I told her who I was and what I was working on.

And then I went for it. I told her, "I have an idea I'd like to run by you. I know your students are looking for real-world experience. What if your next class assignment was to create a logo for Headbands of Hope, and I could pick one to use?"

She paused for a second to think. I waited and waited. My palms grew sweaty until she finally said, "I think that could work. I'll put it on the schedule for next week."

YES! Step two, complete! I had a logo in the works. (High fives!)

The next thing on my Unstoppable Action Plan was to make a website so people could go to HeadbandsofHope.com and buy headbands. I knew I could use an online program, like Shopify, that made starting an e-commerce website easy. But I needed help setting it up. I posted a flyer on the bulletin board where design classes took place. The flyer read, "Designer help needed! Reach out to me if you're willing to help me get my headband business started!" And sure enough, a wonderful student reached out and said she'd love to help me build a website! I had started step three.

We met at the library during lunch every day for one week so she could teach me all the ins and outs of Shopify. And each day, I paid her with a Chipotle burrito. Burritos are a great form of payment! (Just kidding. But seriously, I'd love to be paid in burritos and guacamole now and then.)

Tip

People love helping people. So don't be afraid to ask for help! But when you do, make sure you follow these steps:

1. Introduce yourself and tell them what you're working on.
2. Tell them directly how and why you want their help specifically. The more specific, the better!
3. Recognize that their time is valuable and show them that you appreciate them.

One day she asked me what I was going to work on next after the website was done. I said I had a lot of business questions I needed answers to, like how to register my company, what to charge for each headband, and all the other things that were in the "Hard Things" column of my Unstoppable Action Plan.

"You should meet with Professor Kaye. He teaches Entrepreneurship 101. He can answer all of those questions for you," she shared.

"Really? That's perfect!" I emailed him right then and there.

A few days later, I had a meeting with Professor Kaye, where I went down the "Hard Things" column of my Unstoppable Action Plan and asked him a bunch of questions:

- How do I register my business?
- What are taxes?
- What should I charge for my product?
- How does shipping work?
- Is there anything else I should be doing?

And little by little, Professor Kaye pointed me in the right direction to help me knock out all the tasks I didn't know how to do.

Now, before I go any further in this story, I want to remind you about two super important things:

1. Your age is your superpower!

Being young—and a student—was such an advantage when I started my business. Other students were my first supporters and customers. Teachers were my business mentors. And my school was my business playground where I got access to resources and ideas.

School is not a brick wall to your success. It's a ladder. Your time in school is like a boot camp where you can test ideas and get help for your business or dreams. Headbands of Hope is what it is today *because* I was a student, not in spite of it.

2. Don't let the hard things—the things you don't know how to do—become the reasons why you don't go for your dreams.

Focus on the things you can do, and as you work on those things, you'll learn more about how to do the hard stuff.

Maybe you have an idea for a dog-walking business where you also sell custom dog bandanas to the pet owners. (I would totally be a customer.)

First, you would create a name for your business. Then you would figure out who your ideal customer is. Is it local to your neighborhood? Or do you want to target apartments and condo buildings because they don't have yards for dogs to run around?

> Don't let the hard things become the reasons why you don't go for your dreams.

Then, you would figure out how much you want to charge for your walks and how long you would walk the dogs. This is your product offering!

Once you have some ideas, talk to your parents about it. It's great to show your parents that you've already put some work behind your business idea so they can give you permission (and help) to pursue it.

All my ideas started on a sheet of paper with the permission to do the easy things first. And you can start with the easy stuff too.

Your first draft isn't supposed to be a masterpiece; it's supposed to be a starting point. You don't need the confidence to know *exactly* what you're doing; you just need the confidence to know that you can figure it out!

GO FOR IT

Complete your Unstoppable Action Plan under the "Journal Your Bright Ideas" section. Then choose one of the items under the "Easy Things" list. Start working on it today and give yourself a deadline to complete it.

Journal
YOUR BRIGHT IDEAS

Create an Unstoppable Action Plan to help you take the next steps toward your business or big dreams.

_____ 's Unstoppable Action Plan

(Fill in your name here.)

Easy Things	Hard Things

Remember: Take care of the left side of the list—the easy things—first. You've got this!

CHAPTER TWELVE

Make a Mess

One day after class, I ran to my dorm room with my notebook and a Chipotle burrito. (I can't get enough of those!) I looked at my Unstoppable Action Plan to launch my own business, Headbands of Hope, and sighed. Even though everything in the "Easy Things" column was finished, the first item in the "Hard Things" column was a doozy. I had to figure out how to actually *make* the headbands I was going to sell.

So I met with Professor Kaye, the business professor, and he told me about a website that connected businesses with manufacturers that could make products for you. I stretched out my fingers, typed the website name in Google, and dove into my next internet search.

I opened the website and started going through the entire list of manufacturers that could make products with elastic, which was the only material I knew a headband needs. Each time I found a factory that could make elastic, I reached out to them. And I reached out to *a lot* of factories. Whatever number you're thinking, it was probably more.

I finally got an email back from a person at a factory in Kansas who wanted to discuss the headbands. I was so excited!

I called the factory and told them about my idea: "I want to create a headband company where we donate headbands to kids with illnesses for every headband sold." The person on the phone said they loved the idea and wanted to partner with me. YES!

For about two months, I emailed and called this factory to work on the headband design. I had no design experience, but I created the headband that I would want to wear: thick, colorful, and doesn't slide back on your head.

They said they could make it, but they needed me to pay for all the materials they had to order to make the first set of headbands. So they sent me an invoice for . . .

Ten. Thousand. Dollars.

WHAT?!

That might as well have been the money to buy a private jet with a picture of my dog plastered on the side of it. I was disappointed, but I hadn't given up. I started to do some research to see how I could swing this. I went online and literally typed in the search bar, "How do I get $10,000 to start my business?"

After some digging, two options came up:

1. GET A LOAN FROM THE BANK. You pay them back over time. And because they loaned you the money, you pay them back the amount you borrowed plus more money (a percentage of what you borrowed, also known as *interest*).
2. GET AN INVESTOR IN YOUR BUSINESS. If someone wants to invest in your business, they give you money to start the business, but then they own a percentage of your company in exchange for giving you that money. We call that percentage *equity*.

I wasn't sure which option I should choose, so I talked to my dad about it since he's an entrepreneur too. After telling him the options—get a loan or get an investor—he had an idea.

FUNDING A BUSINESS

Over time, I learned a lot of ways to get funding for a business!

1. Save up your own money if you have a job or allowance. What I didn't know at the time was that you don't actually need a lot to get started!
2. Apply for small business grants. Sometimes schools, local chambers of commerce, and other organizations give out grants to small businesses to help them get started.
3. Create a Kickstarter! This is a website that allows people to buy your product before you start your business. Then when you launch your business, you give them your product—because they already paid for it.
4. Figure it out without funding. Sometimes when we just use what we have, we get creative and come up with an even *better* idea!

"Look," my dad said while reviewing the invoice, my website, and my business plan laid out on the table in front of him. "I think you have a really good idea here. I will be your first investor and give you the $10,000 to start your business."

My jaw dropped.

"And we'll work out a plan for you to pay me back as the business starts to return a profit," he added.

I couldn't believe it. Not only was I thrilled to be getting the money to pay for the headbands, but my *dad* was going to be my investor, which meant he truly believed in my idea and in me.

Now looking back, I realize how privileged I was. My parents

supported me in so many ways. They encouraged me to follow my dreams, and they even gave me the money to start my business. So many people start businesses with no help from friends or family.

I have a friend who sold almost all her belongings at a yard sale to get money to start her business.

I have a friend who started her juice company with a bike and a cooler, and she would bike around selling juice. Now she has a juice shop!

I have a friend who used her time in school to apply for every student grant she could find to start her energy-bite business.

I have a friend who would bake and design cupcakes in her kitchen and bring them to school on people's birthdays. Her cupcakes were so popular that she now caters weddings and sells them in bakeries!

I have a friend who would teach yoga classes in the park. She saved up all the money that people donated for the classes until she could open her own studio. She now has two locations!

Everyone's path to start their business is different. Some people have help, while others don't have access to those same resources. I had a lot of help, and for that I'm truly grateful.

So when I heard my dad's offer, I shook his hand and said, "You have yourself a deal!"

He wrote me a check, and I ran to the bank that same afternoon. It was a Friday, and I wanted the factory to get the money before the weekend so they could start making the headbands first thing on Monday.

I walked into the bank and sent the factory $10,000.

And I never . . .

heard . . .

from them . . .

again.

Yes. You read that correctly. I wired the $10,000 my dad gave me, and the manufacturer never delivered the headbands.

When the factory stopped returning my calls, emails, and other attempts to contact them, I sank into my chair, along with my confidence and hope for the future. What had I done?

Not only was I failing at this business, but I felt like I had failed my dad, the person who trusted me with his money. We even went to court to try to get our money back, but it was gone. And that was one of the toughest pills I've ever had to swallow.

MVP

Have you ever heard the acronym MVP? In sports, it means most valuable player.

But in business, MVP stands for minimum viable product. (*Viable* means working successfully.)

In other words, what's the *least* amount of work you can do for the *lowest* cost to determine if this idea works.

For example, if you want to create a juice shop, don't rent a building before you start making juices. Your MVP is making juices at home that you sell at the farmers' market. Selling the homemade juices at the farmers' market allows you test your product before you spend money on the shop. You'll find out if people like your product, if they want the juices in different containers, if they want different flavors, and more! Then you can improve your product before you spend money on something that customers don't love yet.

In my case, I thought I needed a lot of money to start my business. But if I had just created a small MVP, I could have saved lots of time and dollars!

I started to use this mistake as an excuse to second-guess myself:

Why did you think you could pull this off?

You're clearly not qualified to do this.

You're way out of your league here, or this would not have happened.

You're not meant to be an entrepreneur. Start applying for jobs so you can pay your dad back.

I had a never-ending loop of awful thoughts about myself playing in my head. That voice in our head can use one negative experience (like losing $10,000) as an excuse to say all kinds of negative things about ourselves.

Have you ever messed up and then tried to make it mean something even worse?

Let's say you missed your jump shot during a basketball game. Does that voice in your head say you're not meant to be an athlete and you should just quit the team? Or if you fail a history test, does that voice say *you* are a failure? Or if you try to paint a self-portrait and it turns out looking nothing like you, do you just give up on art altogether?

Sometimes our mind plays tricks on us and tell us who we are based on one teeny, tiny, terrible moment.

But you are much, much more than just a moment in your life. And you know what? **YOU** get to control what that moment means. YOU get to tell that little voice in your head what to think or not think.

And as you keep trying new things, you'll keep messing up. But over time, you'll realize

> Messing up is simply part of the process of learning and creating things.

messing up isn't a reflection of who you are. It's simply part of the process of learning and creating things.

I remember when I realized my dad's money was gone forever. My mind kept asking, *Is this where your great idea ends? Are you calling it quits?*

But when I thought about quitting, my stomach would turn into knots, and I'd think about Renee and all the kids I met during my Make-A-Wish internship who would love to wear headbands after their hair loss.

I didn't want to quit because I knew what I was building was solving a problem. It was scratching an itch.

Do you ever get an itch that drives you *crazy*? It nags and nags you until you finally scratch it.

Think of your ideas like that crazy itch that needs to be scratched.

Your itch is the problem that needs to be solved; your scratch is your solution.

MY ITCH: Kids don't feel good about themselves after losing their hair to chemotherapy.

MY SCRATCH: For each headband sold, Headbands of Hope would provide a headband to a kid with a serious illness.

Okay, your turn. Name your itch (a problem you have or see in the world):

_____

Now name your scratch (your solution):

_____

When you believe that what you're doing is solving a real problem, there's no hurdle too big to stand in your way.

Solving a real problem is more important than the mistakes you make along the way. So give yourself permission to give the wrong answer, make a mess, goof up, and fall down. But then get back up again. Because you're going to fail. A lot. Just like I did. And that's great news! That means you're moving forward and not allowing those failures to stop you from chasing your dream.

> Give yourself permission to give the wrong answer, make a mess, goof up, and fall down. But then get back up again.

I thought people who were successful never failed. Now I know that people who are successful are the ones who know *how* to fail. They view failure as a lesson. They use it as a reason to change and improve and try something different next time. Plus, they get faster and faster at bouncing back after a failure. And the best part of all? They learn how to tell that voice in their head that a mistake is just a part of the creative process. It doesn't make you less valuable as a person.

Because failure is not the opposite of success; it's a part of it.

So just because you don't get a home run every time doesn't mean you stop swinging for the fences.

GO FOR IT

Start seeing every problem as an itch and a scratch. When you feel an itch, ask yourself, "What's the scratch?" By identifying problems and creating solutions, you're training yourself to be an entrepreneur!

Journal

YOUR BRIGHT IDEAS

On average, people have about 6,200 thoughts each day.[1] Write down five negative thoughts you've had about yourself that discourage you from following your dreams.

1.

2.

3.

4.

5.

Now practice controlling the inner voice in your head by replacing those negative thoughts with positive thoughts.

1.

2.

3.

4.

5.

DON'T STOP SWINGING FOR THE FENCES.

CREATE YOUR BRIGHT IDEAS

CHAPTER THIRTEEN

Choose Who You Want to Be

When you really want to do something, you have to choose who you want to be first. Do you want to be the person who *does* the thing or the person who *thought* about doing it? Or the person who *almost* did it? Or the person who *started* it but didn't finish?

You get to choose who you will be:

Founder and CEO of Your Own Ideas	or	Someone Who Had an Idea Once

CIRCLE WHICH ONE YOU WANT TO BE!

After losing the $10,000 my dad gave me, I felt guilty and frustrated for a few weeks, wondering if I was good enough to do this. But I still felt this big itch to help kids. That's why it's so important to believe that what you're doing is solving a problem. Because when times get hard (and they will), you can remember why you started.

I made my choice. I wasn't going to give up and be just someone who had an idea once. I was going to be the founder of Headbands of Hope. I didn't know how yet, but I was going to do it.

A professor told me the business school was giving away $300 grants to students who were starting businesses. After losing $10,000, a $300 grant seemed so small. But it was a starting point!

I applied for the grant and, within a few days, received a congratulations letter saying that I could swing by the office to pick up the check. *Yes!* Then I thought of easy ways I could get the headbands made without spending a lot of money.

I had recently purchased a gift for a friend on Etsy, a website where makers and artists can sell their work. So after I got my grant money, I went to Etsy.com, searched for "headbands," and found a ton of beautiful headband creators. I messaged a few of them and asked if they would partner with me. I told them my plan: they would create and ship the headbands, and I would send them a cut of the sale.

I selected the maker I wanted to partner with, and we decided that we could start with a drop-ship model. A drop-ship model means they make the headband only when the headband is ordered, and then they ship it out. That helped me a ton because I didn't have to spend money on inventory (hundreds of headbands) upfront and ship them myself. I bought three different samples of headbands I wanted to sell, I took pictures of them, and then I posted the pictures to my website on April 25, 2012.

Don't worry, I'll get to

what happened *after* I hit "launch" on my website, but first I want to tell you how important this moment was for me. It was a big step forward on my journey to create a business.

When I met a fork in the road, I could go two different ways: I could turn to the left and decide to give up, or I could go to the right and decide to keep trying. I made the decision to go to the right—to be the person who was going to figure out the hard things. I *chose* to be the founder and CEO of my own ideas.

FOUNDER AND CEO OF YOUR OWN IDEAS

What does it really mean to be the founder and CEO of your own ideas? It means that you go beyond step one (having an idea) to step two (acting on it).

Most people stop at step one because they don't know what to do next or they don't want to fail. But even if you don't know which way to step, at least you're stepping!

When you make that decision, you start to assume that role. You start to *act* how a founder and CEO would act. You start taking charge and solving problems and making big decisions.

But first, you must choose who you want to be. Then you can work toward becoming that version of yourself.

For example, have you ever had cauliflower pasta?

Maybe you think cauliflower is just a vegetable you eat with hummus or ranch dressing. But cauliflower can replace so many things—like bread or pasta—to make a meal healthier.

You want pizza? You can make the crust out of cauliflower.

You like mashed potatoes? No potatoes needed! Just boil and mash cauliflower. And add butter, of course.

Want a side of rice to go with your chicken? You guessed it—cauliflower can be rice too.

Basically, cauliflower can be whatever it wants. You'll probably have the option to build your next home out of cauliflower instead of brick. (Kidding!)

I know it's weird to be inspired by a vegetable. I might be watching too much Food Network, but I truly believe we should have the same attitude as cauliflower. Don't put yourself in one category. I bet a sweet potato never knew it could turn into chips or that a tortilla and a hard-shell taco could be glued together with cheese to become the best of both worlds: crunchy and soft.

I'm sure you're probably thinking, *Okay, Jess, we get it. You have a weird fascination with cauliflower. What does this have to do with creating my own ideas?*

Just like cauliflower can be whatever it wants to be, so can you.

Sometimes we feel stuck, like we can't try new things.

Maybe you've played the piano since you were four, but now you want to play the violin. Or you're really good at playing basketball, but now you want to try painting a beautiful picture. Or maybe you've always been the shy one among your friends, but you want to try being bolder.

> Don't put yourself in one category.

You are not one thing. You are *so many* things, and you're constantly growing and changing. You don't have to stay the same. The more you do, the more you learn about who you are and what you want to try next.

When I decided I was going to be the CEO of my ideas, I launched Headbands of Hope with just a small $300 grant—while still owing my dad $10,000.

Being CEO of your own ideas does *not* mean getting it right the first time, making lots of money, or even having your own business card. It means believing these three things:

1. No matter my age or where I am, I have the power to make a difference.
2. When I discover problems, I'm brave and courageous enough to try to solve them—even if it takes a few tries!
3. I learn through action. The more I act on my solutions and ideas, the more I learn.

If you believe these three things about yourself, then you are the founder and CEO of your own ideas.

GO FOR IT

Put on your CEO hat this week. For each activity you do, follow these important steps:

1. Believe that you can make a difference.
2. Know that you can solve problems.
3. Learn through action!

And see where the CEO mind-set takes you!

Journal
YOUR BRIGHT IDEAS

If cauliflower can be pizza crust, pasta, and just about anything else, what can you be? Write down or draw out all the things you want to become (painter, business owner, comedian, boss, or something else!).

BE WHOEVER YOU WANT to BE

CREATE YOUR BRIGHT IDEAS

CHAPTER FOURTEEN

Replace Worry with Wonder

After I hit "launch" on my website, I sent out an email to my entire family (my parents, aunts, uncles, cousins, and grandparents).

Hi, family!

I wanted to let you know that I launched my business, Headbands of Hope. For every headband sold, one is given to a child with cancer. I would love it if you checked out the website and spread the word to anyone you know!

Love,
Jess

A few minutes after I sent that email, I saw a Shopify notification: "*Ca-ching!* You have a sale."

My heart started pounding. *A sale! My first sale!* Someone went to my website and paid me actual money for something I created. I clicked on the notification immediately.

Order #0001: Laurie Ekstrom. Cornelius, NC. Chiffon Flower in Red.

Oh. That's my mom. Moms don't count as customers! Within seconds I had an email from her:

So proud of you, sweetie! Can't wait to get my chiffon flower headband!

Love, Mom

I could feel my confidence deflate as I watched each minute pass by and no more orders came in. My mind started to race with doubts.

What if this was a bad idea?

What if I priced my product too high? What if people don't like the headbands?

What if all of this was for nothing?

What if? What if? What if?

Has your mind ever gotten stuck in a loop of negative what-ifs? *What if I don't make the team? What if I don't know anyone there? What if I don't make any friends? What if I'm not good enough?*

Anytime our future is uncertain (which is 100 percent of the time!), our mind tries to focus on what-ifs. And it usually gets stuck on the *negative* what-ifs instead of the positive ones.

Whenever this happens to me, I remind myself of one thing:

IF WE CAN WORRY ABOUT THE FUTURE, THEN WE CAN ALSO IMAGINE A BETTER ONE.

The muscle we use to worry is the same one we use to wonder. And that's great news!

So when you're stuck on a negative what-if loop, pause. Then replace your worries with positive, encouraging, imaginative wonder.

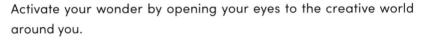

STEP INTO WONDER!

Activate your wonder by opening your eyes to the creative world around you.

- Go outside and look at the clouds.
- Go on a hike and see what you notice about nature.
- Start painting a picture with no plan.
- Talk to a friend.

The more you can surround yourself with the beauty around you, the more you can increase your positive wonder.

Go ahead. Try it now! Come up with as many positive what-ifs as you can.

What if . . .

_____

_____

_____

When I had made only one headband sale (to my mom!), I changed my negative what-ifs to positive ones:

What if people are just wanting to learn more about Headbands of Hope before they decide to buy a headband?

What if I'm just getting started on something amazing?

What if I'm doing exactly what I need to be doing for my business?

If there's one thing I learned during this slow beginning, it's this: just because something is slow doesn't mean it isn't moving forward.

I'll be honest with you: your ideas aren't going to spread like wildfire in the beginning. I hope they do, but most of the time, they won't. You may have to strike a match again and again before your little flames turn into a big fire.

You may experience some uncomfortable moments after you start your business or take the first steps toward your big dream. It may seem like no one cares about what you're doing. But that's when the real dreams and businesses are built. If it were easy, then everyone would do it, right?

You create your *best* work after you make changes and improve and try new things. That beginning season is tough, and the people who are just looking for a quick win will eventually quit. Success comes to those who stick around and keep trying to make their business or dream even better.

> Success comes to those who stick around and keep trying.

If you launch your idea and it's not getting the attention you want, ask yourself these questions:

1. Am I putting too much pressure on myself?

_____

_____

2. What are the small wins I've had so far? How can I celebrate those wins?

_____

_____

3. Who will give me an honest opinion of my business or dream and tell me what they would do differently?

_____

_____

4. How can I get more people to see what I'm doing?

_____

5. Who are my ideal customers or supporters? Where are they? How can I tell them about my business or dream?

_____

_____

Tip

Start by asking your parents who they know who might be able to help you with your idea.

Then, ask your teachers, your friends, your coaches, or other members of your community for help.

You can say something like, "Hi! I'm working on creating a business that [insert your business idea here]. Do you have any tips for me on ways I can get the word out?"

Answering these questions can turn your worry into wonder because they remind you that your journey isn't over. There's still hope. There's still more to do and try. I knew my business wouldn't survive if my mom was my only customer, which meant there was more I needed to do and try. So I tackled questions 4 and 5.

I had a monthly subscription to a magazine called *Fitness,* and it was sitting on the kitchen counter. I realized that my ideal customer was probably someone who likes fitness because athletic people wear headbands. I wondered if something in the magazine could push me in the right direction.

I flipped it open and started skimming the pages. I saw recipes, workout routines, and inspiring stories. Then I stopped on an article titled "Five Fitness Bloggers to Watch."

I started reading about each blogger. *Hmmm,* I thought. *Maybe I could see if these bloggers would wear my headbands to help me spread the word?*

I opened my computer and typed in each blogger's website listed in the magazine article. I found their email addresses and emailed all five bloggers, asking if they'd like to work with me. I told them I would ship them free headbands so they could talk about them on their blog.

Out of the five bloggers, two replied. And one of them said yes.

This was another lesson for me. Reach out to as many people as you can because you never know who will say yes!

I shipped some headbands to the blogger who agreed to work with me. A few weeks later, she posted about my headbands, and I got $500 worth of orders from complete strangers.

I exhaled. *I think this is going to work.*

GO FOR IT

Start thinking about who you know: your parents, your parents' friends, your teachers, your neighbors, your friends, and your friends' parents. Starting with your parents, talk to five people this week about your idea. The more you talk to people about your big dream, business plan, or world-changing idea, the more people will help you with it.

Journal
YOUR BRIGHT IDEAS

List things you can do to spread the word about your dreams or business. Don't think. Just write whatever comes to your mind first! Then circle five things you plan to do this week.

CHAPTER FIFTEEN

Choose Inspiration

When I was in middle school, I was taller than most of the kids in my class, even the boys. When we'd play basketball at recess, they'd always pick me to do the jump ball at the beginning of the game, and I'd get so embarrassed. I would look at the other girls in my class and wish that I could have their small height and frame.

But when you're spending time wishing you looked or acted like someone else, you're not valuing your unique strengths and individuality. Being tall has so many perks. But I spent so much time wishing I was shorter that I didn't take advantage of my unique height.

Even into adulthood, I've struggled a lot with comparison. I scroll through picture after picture of my friends on social media until I officially feel like I'll never measure up to everyone else.

I'm behind and will never catch up. I'll never look like that. I wish I could make jokes as funny as hers.

I spend so much energy trying to be someone else that I don't have enough energy to be myself.

So even after bloggers started writing about Headbands of Hope and we started to get some media attention, I would walk the aisles of Target and say, "Why can you buy other brands of headbands here but not mine?" Or I'd open Instagram and see someone else's business celebrating a huge milestone and feel a sharp pang of jealousy.

Why did they get selected for that TV show and not me? Why is this business making more money than mine? How is she doing collaborations with Selena Gomez and I can't even pay myself yet?

Comparing yourself to others makes you feel like you need to be doing what everyone else is doing. *What if I don't enjoy dancing like all the other girls in my grade? (I'd rather be the DJ!) Should I be taking selfies? (I'd rather take pictures of nature!)*

It's hard to remember how awesome you are when all you can think about is how awesome someone else is. Your grades need to be like theirs. Your outfit needs to be like theirs. Your hashtags need to be like theirs. Your cupcake needs to have sprinkles like theirs.

Social media makes it *so easy* to compare yourself with others. But the reality is, social media is the tiniest fraction of a person's life. Most people only post about the good times, not the times when stuff went wrong.

I'm guilty of this too. I didn't post a picture of myself when I lost the $10,000 loan from my dad. Instead, I posted a picture of myself on stage at a speaking engagement with the lights shining perfectly on my blazer and heels.

During the first few months after I started my business, my anxiety was at an all-time high because I was focused on what other people were thinking and saying about me. But I should have been focused on what *I* thought about me. Because if I really looked at the whole scene of starting a business that helps kids with cancer, I should have taken the time to give myself a proud pat on the back. Instead, I was too busy wondering if other people were proud of me.

When we compare ourselves to others, a few not-so-great things happen:

- We question our own instincts.
- We feel less than.
- We feel like we're always a few steps behind where we should be.
- We try to be or create something that already exists!

But here's the thing. Instead of comparing yourself to others, you can choose to be *inspired* by them instead.

When we're inspired by others, great things happen:

Tip

You're allowed to compare yourself to one person and one person only.

Yourself!

Have I improved? Am I better than I was yesterday? Am I making progress? Am I learning more?

Those are all great questions to ask yourself and realize how far you've come.

- We can see new possibilities for our future.
- We're still confident in ourselves and our goals and dreams.
- We have proof of what's possible for us.
- We can genuinely root for other people to succeed.
- We can think of new ideas for ourselves.

Now, which one sounds better to you: comparison or inspiration?

Comparison steals your time, your hopes, your dreams, and your self-worth.

Think of a time when you compared yourself to someone else. What thoughts went through your head? Example: "I can't believe she got an A on the science test and I got a B. She's smart, and I'm not!"

———

———

Okay, now remember that same situation, but instead of comparing yourself to that person, imagine that you were inspired by them. How would you act differently? Example: "Wow, she really knows her science! That's impressive. I'm going to ask her to study together for the next test because I can learn a lot from her!"

———

———

Even though my business was just getting started, the biggest challenge I had was not how well my website was running or how much money I had in the bank. It was my own mind. I was letting myself fall into these comparison traps. So I had to train myself to stop comparing myself to others and start being inspired by them instead.

Maybe you started your business a month ago and someone who *just* got started a week ago is making more sales than you. It would be easy to say, "Their business is better than mine!" But maybe they're making sales but not making any profit. You have no idea!

Or maybe you've been in gymnastics for two months, but someone who just joined your class can already do a handstand. You think, *She's so good at gymnastics! I should just give up.* But maybe that girl can't balance on the balance beam like you can. Or maybe she doesn't practice often, and if you stick with it, you'll soon be the best in your class.

> Don't lose the beauty of what makes you unique.

Remember that you never know the full story, so you can't make giant assumptions about yourself or someone else based on a moment of comparison.

It took practice, but it changed the way I look at other people's photos on social media or how I feel about people who seem to have it all together. Now I know that there's room for everyone at the top, so I don't need to compare myself with them or compete with them.

In fact, when you're so focused on being like *them* (whoever *they* are), you lose the beauty of what makes you unique. Simply put, you lose being *you.*

GO FOR IT

When you're tempted to compare yourself to someone else, stop the comparison trap by complimenting that person instead. Then remind yourself of a strength you have. You'll feel good about that person and yourself!

Journal
YOUR BRIGHT IDEAS

Write about someone who inspires you. This could be a friend, a teacher, or even a celebrity you don't know. Resist the urge to compare yourself to them and instead write about what you like about that person.

When You Try To Be Like Someone Else, You Lose the Magic of Being You.

CREATE YOUR BRIGHT IDEAS

CHAPTER SIXTEEN

Do What's Worth Failing For

A few years after I started my business, Headbands of Hope, I decided to take my chances and go to a trade show in Atlanta. A trade show is where brands and products (like mine) set up booths in a big convention center so that stores from all over the world can come and choose products to carry.

I wanted to get my headbands into stores, so I saved up $5,000 for the registration fee, packed my bags, and went to Atlanta.

As soon as I got there, I regretted going. All the other booths had professionally made signs, spinning store displays, TV screens running commercials of their product, and multiple people with clipboards and iPads ready to take orders. I had a plastic banner I'd purchased for twenty dollars and a dozen jars I had spray-painted, which I slid the headbands onto to create a "fancy" display. Needless to say, I felt out of my league.

To make matters worse, when I looked at the map of the convention center to see where my booth was located, I couldn't even find it. It was *behind* the bathrooms. I was by myself with no foot traffic of customers walking by.

The show began, and I stood in my booth with my clipboard and boxes of headbands, feeling like I had just poured $5,000 down the drain. The show was three days long, and by day three, I still hadn't written a single order or even talked to a potential customer.

As I stood in the booth wondering if I should just leave early, I watched customers walk through the other aisles. I was close enough to read their name tags, which included the name of their store.

I saw one woman walking, and her name tag read *Senior Buyer, Ulta Beauty.*

In that moment, I felt a jolt of energy spark through my body. Ulta Beauty?! They carry so many hair accessories! They have a thousand locations. Getting my headbands into this chain of stores would be a dream come true!

I watched her walk farther and farther away. I wanted to chase after her, but I felt like my feet were cemented to the ground with fear.

Have you ever felt like that? There's something you want to do or someone you want to talk to, or you have the urge to speak up, but then, suddenly, doubt stops you in your tracks.

I like to call this

experience a *cement-feet moment*: when your heart is telling you to go for it, but your mind is saying, *Not so fast! Think about all the things that could go wrong!*

And, sure, things could go wrong. I knew that if I chased down that Ulta Beauty buyer, she could call security on me. She could reject me. She could tell me my headbands aren't good enough. She could tell me to stop wasting my time on this silly business idea. All those outcomes were possibilities. And, if all those things happened, I'd live to tell about it and still be standing exactly where I was. Behind the bathrooms.

You may have heard this question before: "What would you do if you knew you couldn't fail?"

I like to take the opposite approach and ask, "What is worth failing for?"

FEAR OF FAILURE

When people have a fear of failure, they get in a bad habit of making sure they fail before they even try. Like if you're afraid of failing your science test, you may not study the night before. That way, you have an excuse for why you failed. This is called a *self-fulfilling prophecy*.

But you can break this habit! Tell someone about a failure you've had and what you learned from it.

When you don't hide from your failures and instead embrace them as important lessons, you become stronger and stronger—and that's what leads to success!

What would you do if you knew that failure was a possibility but it was worth the shot anyway? That's the real question. Failure is always a possible outcome, but that doesn't mean it's a reason not to try.

So, really, having cement feet boils down to a simple math equation:

Is the potential reward greater than the impact of failing?

In other words, if I fail, I'll be standing right where I am now. So the impact of failure is nothing but a bruised ego. But if the Ulta Beauty buyer says yes and Headbands of Hope gets into Ulta stores, then that is a *huge* win for the future of the business.

So what do you think I did? If you guessed that I went for it, you are correct! Literally. I started running through the booths after this woman with the Ulta Beauty name tag.

What is worth failing for?

When I finally got to her, I was sweaty, I was out of breath, and I did not give the best sales pitch I've ever given. But I also remember I took the headband off my head and gave it to her to keep. Why not? I also gave her a thumb drive with our catalog on it and told her it had all my contact info on it if she'd like to discuss placing an order.

She politely brushed me off, thanked me for the headband, and continued walking.

I walked back to my booth, headband-less, and thought about what just happened. I didn't feel discouraged. Instead, I felt empowered. Why was I hiding behind this bathroom the whole trade show when I could be out there talking to people? I immediately signed up for the next trade show (but in a different booth location, of course).

This moment taught me something I'll never forget:

FAILURE WILL ALWAYS FEEL BETTER THAN REGRET.

No matter the outcome, it will always feel better to go for it and have a story to tell than wonder what could have been. If you try to sell your hand-painted mugs but realize it takes too much time for not enough money, then you may want to move on to another idea—and that's great! That is wonderful news because you tried something, and even though it didn't work, you now have a story you can learn from for your next idea.

When I was a kid, I once stood in line for three hours to audition for the show *All That.* I had no acting experience. I just saw an opportunity and went for it. I'm sure this story would be a lot cooler if I could tell you I got on the show, but I didn't. However, I could watch that show in peace knowing that I tried, instead of watching and wondering, *What if I had stood in that line and given it a shot?*

Oh, and one more thing. Four years after that first trade show, Headbands of Hope was in all one thousand Ulta Beauty stores.

GO FOR IT

Whenever you think, *But what if I mess up?* or *But what if it doesn't work out?*, think about what it would feel like to never know the answer. It doesn't feel great!

Instead, switch those thoughts with these: *But what if it* does *work out?* or *Either way, I'll learn something!* or *No matter the outcome, I'll be glad I tried!*

Journal
YOUR BRIGHT IDEAS

What is worth failing for? What is something you're so passionate or excited about that even if it doesn't work out, you'll be glad you tried it?

Failure will always feel better than regret

CREATE YOUR BRIGHT IDEAS

CHAPTER SEVENTEEN

Show Up

I have a secret trick that has helped me build my business and follow my dreams. It feels silly and simple, but it works! You don't need any special skills, you don't need to know a new language, and you don't need any special materials (other than yourself).

The secret is only two words: **SHOW. UP.**

Yup, that's it. Show up. By showing up and putting yourself out in the world instead of sitting at home behind a computer or TV, you increase the probability of great things happening to you.

When I was in middle school, I was a huge Charlotte Hornets basketball fan. Every game, they'd pick kids to make a tunnel on the court, and the team would run through the tunnel and high-five the kids as each player was announced. I knew they had to pick the kids before the game, so I told my dad I wanted to get to the stadium early.

We got there an hour before the game started, and no one was there except for the staff setting up! We walked around the stadium until a man in a purple Hornets polo walked up to us and said to me, "Hey, kid, would you like to introduce the Hornets tonight?"

I looked up at my dad, and we high-fived. Then I was taken backstage to get a cool new T-shirt and wait to be brought out onto the court.

By just showing up, I put myself on the path of possibilities.

So when I started my business, I didn't do everything by myself at home alone. I joined a coworking space with other entrepreneurs. By showing up there every day, I met incredible people who helped me with my business and became my close friends.

One time I was asked on a Tuesday if I wanted to go to a conference that Friday. I didn't know anything about the conference, but I said yes because I knew that just by being there, something great could happen. And it did! I met so many people I was inspired by and later worked with.

Another time I applied to compete in an entrepreneurship competition at Under Armour. I didn't win anything, but just by being there, things happened. I formed a partnership with Under Armour, where they repurposed their unused fabrics into headbands that my company donated to children's hospitals!

Sometimes I catch myself wanting to hibernate—to work on my business at home alone, then watch Netflix and do the same thing again tomorrow. But when we stay in our safe little bubbles, we miss the chance for good things to happen. If your passion is bird-watching, the only way to find birds is to be outside where they might by flying around.

When you stay at home, you're not making any room for positive collisions.

Positive collisions are chance moments when you put yourself out there and something good happens. Maybe you participate in your school's spelling bee, and while you're there, the governor makes an appearance. Then you get a chance to meet them, and you ask to volunteer at their office—and they say yes! Wouldn't that be cool?

Or maybe you're at a track meet, and you meet someone from another school who becomes your future business partner and best friend.

Anything is possible when you show up. You can't just wait for things to happen to you. You have to open yourself up to new experiences. You have to get on the path of possibilities.

IDEAS FOR SHOWING UP

1. Ask your parents if you can join an after-school club, sport, or group that interests you.
2. Go for walks around your neighborhood and find your favorite trees and flowers.
3. At school, try to sit with new people every day at lunch instead of just your friends.

Any chance you can be outside, try new things, and meet new people, you are putting yourself on the path of possibilities!

When you go to a basketball game and the mascot comes out with the T-shirt gun that fires into the stands, do you ever see the person quietly sitting with their hands in their lap catch a T-shirt? No! The person standing on their seat with their hands in the air and their face painted with a target gets the shirt—and appears on the jumbotron.

Get on the path of possibilities.

That's because they're *calling for it.* They're putting themselves on the path of possibilities. They're increasing their chances by saying what they want and positioning themselves to receive it.

Whenever I cook in the kitchen, my dog sits right beside me. I'd like to think it's because he loves me so much, but unfortunately, that's not it. He's just hoping I'll drop something, and he'll be there to eat it. It doesn't happen every time I cook, but his chances of getting the food will always be higher when he's in the kitchen versus when he's on the couch.

My friend Emily *always* wins concert tickets on radio stations. At least once a month she's attending some event that she won front-row tickets to, even if she doesn't know the band. People always say, "Wow, Emily, you're so lucky! You win all the time!" But I know the truth behind her luck—because there is none. She just calls *all the time*. Whenever there's a contest, she'll enter it. So she doesn't win because she's lucky. She wins because she puts herself in the running *every time*. She's bound to get a few wins every now and then.

YOU'RE SO LUCKY

Did you know you can *create* your own luck?

For example, Beethoven lost his hearing, but he created some of the greatest musical works of all time *after* he lost his hearing![1]

Here's how you can create your own luck:

- Search for or create new opportunities.
- Listen to your gut.
- Dream of success and try to fulfill that dream.
- Work hard at what you want to achieve.

That's what we should do when creating a business, following our dreams, or becoming a world-changer. To become a part of something, we have to put ourselves on the path of possibilities.

Get involved in extracurricular activities. Talk to your teachers and parents about your dreams. Introduce yourself to new people. And apply for the things you want.

I have a friend who wanted to be a motivational speaker. She attended a conference, and the speaker called in sick. So she offered to speak in his place. And the conference coordinators said yes! **BOOM!** She just landed the biggest speaking engagement of her life because she showed up.

Remember, you can't get picked to play in the game if you're not *at* the game. Show up and put yourself on the path of possibilities.

GO FOR IT

Do you usually sit with the same kids at lunch? This week, sit with someone new every day or introduce yourself to a kid you've never met before. Ask them questions and get to know them!

Journal
YOUR BRIGHT IDEAS

List activities, events, or ideas where you can start showing up.

Get on the path of possibilities.

CHAPTER EIGHTEEN

Don't Wait for Instant Success

After I started Headbands of Hope, I realized that a great way to spread the word about my business was by telling my story through speaking engagements. I started speaking at schools, events, companies, and conferences about how I started Headbands of Hope and how we should all believe in our ideas.

After I spoke at one event with a lot of fancy-name speakers, the main speaker (a *very* successful founder of a company we've all heard of; let's call him "Bill") came up to me.

"Do you have a valid passport?"

Caught off guard, I responded, "Yes. I think so."

"Good," he replied, "because I'm going to make you a world-class speaker."

We exchanged our contact information, and he said his agent was going to call me and set me up with speaking engagements all over the world. *Say what?!*

I ran out of the venue and couldn't dial my parents fast enough.

"Mom! Mom! You won't believe it. I met *Bill*, and he believes in my speaking! He said he's going to send me all over the world for speaking engagements!"

We did a happy dance on the phone, and then I ran back to my apartment to check the expiration date on my passport.

Then I waited for Bill and his agent to call. I waited. And waited. I even followed up and then waited some more. And then some more.

Nothing ever happened. And for a while, I thought I missed my only opportunity to be successful. I believed *he* was my golden ticket to the train of success and that my golden ticket had slipped through my fingertips.

Have you ever felt that way before? Like your one shot to do something somehow passed you by?

Write down a moment when you felt like you lost your shot at something important:

After months passed, I was bummed that I had never heard from Bill, but I didn't stop speaking. I kept putting my name in the hat for events, I worked on my message, and any chance I had the opportunity to get in front of people to share my story (even for free), I did it.

Years went by, and I spoke at more and more events, and the stages and audiences got bigger and bigger.

Then, about five years after I first met Bill, I ran into him at a conference where *I* was the main speaker. My face was on the pamphlets, the billboards, and the shiny posters.

"Jess! Did my agent ever get in touch with you? I need to get her on that," Bill said when he approached me, shaking my hand.

"No, she didn't," I said. "But don't even worry about it, Bill. I'm good."

Here's the thing: I thought for a long time that Bill's help was the only way I was going to become successful, that I had to wait for the "golden ticket" phone call that would solve all my problems and give me instant success. But there is

Did You Know?

Did you know that Walt Disney's school newspaper editor said he didn't have imagination or any good ideas?

Did you know Albert Einstein didn't start speaking until he was four years old or start reading until he was seven?

Did you know that a lot of publishers rejected the Harry Potter series before it was finally published?[1]

Many successful people didn't succeed instantly. They had to keep trying before they finally made it!

no single person or moment that is your golden ticket. **YOU** are your only golden ticket.

Over the years, I've thought many moments, people, and opportunities were going to be my golden

YOU are your
only golden ticket.

ticket. I thought, *If only I can get on* this *television show! If only I could partner with* this *company! If only I can meet with* this *person!* Then *I'll be set.*

A lot of those meetings happened. And a lot of them didn't. But none of them determined my future or my success. Only I can do that.

So there's good news and bad news to all of this.

The bad news is that no train is going to stop at your station and give you instant success.

The good news is that your golden ticket is in your hands right now. It's your *consistency* to show up, keep trying, and get better and better at your craft.

Tip

Write a plan for when and where you want to work on your dreams. Before school? After school? What do you want to accomplish each day? Write it all down to keep yourself on track!

So don't wait for a "golden ticket" moment of success.

Your success won't be one TikTok video that goes viral or one award that you win. Those things have happened to me, and I still had to wake up and work the next day!

Your success will be the *sum* of all your small moments. Every single time you work on your dream, it's like you're putting a quarter in your piggy bank. It doesn't feel like a lot at the time, but one day your piggy bank will be overflowing with quarters!

GO FOR IT

Make a list of all the small things you do this week that will help you reach your goals and dreams. At the end of the week, give yourself a pat on the back and realize that all your small actions will lead to something big!

Journal
YOUR BRIGHT IDEAS

Look back at your answer on page 152, where you wrote about losing your shot at something important. What can you do to keep trying for that goal without waiting for instant success?

CHAPTER NINETEEN

Follow Your North Star

When I was a kid, teachers would say that we should "find our purpose."

Where is it? Under the couch? Tucked away in my closet? In my laundry basket next to my dirty socks? What does it look like? Is it round or square? Red or blue? I don't even know what I'm looking for!

I would try a new hobby, like volleyball, and after practice I'd think, *Is this my purpose?*

Or I would get a good grade on a school paper about saving manatees and think, *Is saving manatees my purpose?*

I was never sure if the things I enjoyed or the things I was good at were automatically my *purpose* in life.

But one day I saw people on the beach using metal detectors to skim over the sand. When their metal detector beeped, they dug in the sand to see if they'd found gold or just a paper clip. And I realized that using a metal detector is what it's like to search for purpose. Skimming the sand with a metal detector is like engaging with the world, trying new things, and putting yourself out there. And every once in a while, you'll hear a beep. You've found something! If it's something that interests you, that gives you that warm, fuzzy feeling, and that makes you think, *Hey, I like doing this,* then it's gold! So when you hear that beep, take notice and pursue that thing to see if it could be your purpose.

After starting Headbands of Hope, I heard the metal detector beeping. I got the warm and fuzzy feeling. I knew why I was waking up every day. I knew every small thing I did for my business led to a bigger mission of helping kids with cancer. That's purpose, right? When you find something that you like to do and that helps others too, **BOOM!** Say hello to purpose!

A few years after I'd started my business, that warm, fuzzy feeling was still there, but I started to get an itch too. No, not an itch that leaves a nasty rash that you need a special cream for. But an itch of curiosity. The more I learned about the world through the eyes of my business, the more I wondered about my bigger place in it. I started to itch to do brand-new things:

- To speak on stages
- To write books
- To help women with what I'd learned
- To solve *other* problems I'd uncovered as I grew my business

This felt uncomfortable to me (like any itch does!). I thought, *Haven't I already found my purpose by starting Headbands of Hope? So why do I have an itch to do other things?*

But I realized that purpose is not a role, title, or thing you do. Your purpose is actually the answer to the question "*Why* do I want to do this?"

For me, the answer to this question was "I love helping people be confident."

And I realized that I could help people be confident in a bunch of different ways—yes, by providing headbands to kids who have hair loss, but also by writing books, teaching courses, and talking on stages about my story.

My purpose is what guided me to the different things I wanted to do. It's like the North Star.

THE NORTH STAR

Draw yourself on a boat with the North Star above you. What does the North Star stand for? What are you rowing toward?

The North Star is unique because the North Pole (the north axis of the earth) is pointed almost directly at it, which means that, as the earth spins, the North Star appears to remain in the same spot while the other stars circle around it. And because sailors can use the North Star to find north, they have used this special star to navigate their voyages for centuries.

> Purpose is not *what* you do; it's *why* you do it.

But no one has ever arrived at the North Star because that's impossible. They've only used it for guidance.

And that's how purpose works. Purpose is an idea that shines brightly above you and can guide you to a new adventure.

Your purpose is not *what* you do; it's *why* you do it. For example, maybe it's your dream to be a veterinarian. Your purpose is not being a vet. It's helping animals that can't help themselves. Or maybe your dream is to start a hip-hop dance class. Your purpose isn't being a dancer. It's helping people discover themselves through dance.

If purpose isn't our actions but rather our reasoning *behind* our actions, then you may do a bunch of different things—and they're all purposeful.

Since I started Headbands of Hope in 2012, I've done a lot of different things because of my purpose to help people become confident:

- I've become a speaker, traveling all over the world.
- I've become an author, writing this book for you in addition to my book for grown-ups called *Chasing the Bright Side*.
- I started a business called Mic Drop Workshop that helps women become speakers and authors.
- I created a journaling app called Prompted.io for self-improvement.

Tip

Write down *everything* you're interested in, even your smaller hobbies or your favorite books or shows. Sometimes our interests have common themes. And everything that you love to do, watch, or read gives you information about what your purpose is!

Now it's your turn. Write down your dream, business idea, or world-changing goal, as well as all the things that interest you right now:

_____

_____

_____

_____

_____

_____

_____

_____

_____

_____

_____

_____

If you had to pick one common theme out of what you wrote above, what would it be? Do they all revolve around animals? Do they all revolve around helping people? Does your list revolve around saving the environment? Or something else?

_____

_____

_____

_____

_____

_____

Now let's show how that common theme can help other people (because your purpose is always going to be bigger than you). Fill in these blanks:

Hi, my name is _____ ,

(Fill in your name here.)

and through my _____

(Fill in your dream, business idea, or
world-changing goal here.)

I help people _____ .

(Fill in one way you'll help people here.)

Meaning and purpose are unique to each person. So what might be meaningful to you might not be to someone else. Your purpose is yours and only yours.

Now, you might be asking, "What if I still don't know what my purpose is?"

My answer would be "Join the club!" A lot of people need time to find their purpose.

So keep putting yourself out there. Keep solving problems. And keep following your North Star.

GO FOR IT

This week, think about what you enjoy doing. Then ask yourself, *Why do I love these things? What is it about this activity that makes me excited?*

When you can discover why you love things, you learn about your greater purpose!

YOUR BRIGHT IDEAS

What is your North Star? Is there a cause you care a lot about? Is there something you like to help people do or learn? What is a mission that's important to you that guides your dreams and decisions?

CHAPTER TWENTY

Pick Your Song

ave you ever had poison ivy? It's so itchy and miserable!

Okay, so you're probably thinking, *Jess, what does poison ivy have to do with anything?* Well, I'm about to tell you.

In 1962, there was a study in Japan where people were exposed to poison ivy. Doctors rubbed poison ivy on one arm of each participant, but they told the patients that it was just a regular leaf. Then they rubbed a regular leaf on each participant's other arm, but they told them it was poison ivy. So sneaky!

Here's the crazy part. All but two people experienced an allergic reaction to the *regular* leaf! And they didn't react at all to the poison ivy.[1] *Say what?!*

Now, I'm not saying poison ivy isn't poisonous, but what I *am* saying is that maybe we don't give our brains enough credit. If our brains are strong enough to choose how our skin will react or not to react to a poisonous (or not poisonous) leaf, then they're definitely strong enough to choose our mood and energy for the day.

Several years ago I was backstage at a conference in Indiana getting ready to speak to three thousand college students from all over the country when one of the backstage staff members asked a question that threw me off.

"Hey, Jess, what song do you want to walk out to?" he asked.

"What do you mean?" I responded.

"The song. We play a song as you walk out onto the stage," he clarified. "What song do you want it to be?"

I paused for a minute. It wasn't abnormal for them to play music as I walked out on stage. I just had never been asked what song *I* wanted them to play.

"A Bruno Mars song," I said.

"Got it," he said, and he put his headset back on.

My husband took me to a Bruno Mars concert one year for my birthday when we were dating. We were broke college kids, so our tickets were for the nosebleed section. But that didn't matter to me. The way I was dancing, I may as well have been one of Bruno's backup dancers on stage. My husband had to move down a couple of seats so I could have more range of motion. Something about his songs made me feel like I had wings, and everyone needed to watch out because I was about to fly.

I was standing backstage at my speaking gig waiting for my cue to enter when the guy said, "Now!" and motioned me to move onto the stage.

As I took my first step into the bright lights, the song started playing, and I felt more confident than Ariana Grande doing singing impersonations. I was unstoppable. The music faded, and then I gave one of the best talks I've ever delivered. Afterward, I couldn't help but keep replaying that question in my head: *What song do you want to walk out to?*

Okay, so it's not every day that someone is going to blast a cool song while you walk out onstage to a cheering crowd. But what if when you wake up, you pick the song you want to start the day with? Think about your morning—your alarm goes off, you put your feet on the ground, you walk to the bathroom, and you brush your teeth. For me, that's the moment when I'm looking in the mirror, thinking through my schedule for the day. And that's when I decide what my "song" is going to be, because we always have a choice for how we're going to approach our day.

> You pick the song you want to start the day with.

We pick the lyrics, the chorus, and the tempo. We get to pick if we walk out to Bruno Mars, Olivia Rodrigo, a techno track with dope bass drops, or a slow, sad song about a breakup.

Imagine you were in a bad mood at school or started losing steam at a sports practice, and you thought to yourself, *I'm done trying.* But then a song starts playing, and with that first beat, you change too. And whatever task is in front of you doesn't seem so tough anymore. Now you're ready to go harder than Simone Biles doing her floor routine. Before you know it, that tough thing is just a warm-up for what you're about to do next.

Now, here's the crazy part: we control the music we play in our head and in our life. With every challenge we face, with every new beginning, with every win or lose, and with every new day, we pick the song—our tone, pace, and attitude toward the day. You choose if you get the poison ivy rash or if you walk away unscathed.

MAKE PLAYLISTS

A playlist can help you choose the mood you want to be in. So make a playlist for every occasion: when you need encouragement to keep going, when you want to feel extra happy, or when you want something to pump you up to do something big!

Tap on these playlists when you need them.

We don't always have to be at the highest tempo and happiest notes, but we control how we react to each moment of the day because we control the playlist. Choosing your song means that you get to choose how you react each moment. Maybe one day you play a loud hip-hop playlist while you're working on your business, asking your friends and teachers for feedback, and going shopping with your parents and getting business inspiration in the stores.

And then maybe the next day you play something soft and quiet to recharge your energy, reflect on your week, and journal about what's to come. But always remember, we control the playlist to our own lives.

We get lost by believing we're not in control of our own melody. We believe our song is stuck on a loop, and we can't hit "Next." So much of life is not just the experience, whether good or bad, but the choices we make after an experience—like the song we pick as we move forward, go left or right, or say yes or no. Maybe you're stuck on a moment that happened in band rehearsals last week where you messed up a song on the violin and had to start over. You can't stop thinking about it! But do you remember when you didn't even know how to *hold* a violin? It's so easy to play your problems on a loop in your brain instead of focusing on how far you've come!

Now it's your turn. You're the DJ of your day.
What song makes you feel like you can do anything?

_____

Turn on that song and then finish these sentences with the first things that come to mind.

I am a _____ person.

I was born to _____ .

My favorite part about myself is _____ .

I know I'm going to be successful because _____ .

My alter-ego nickname for myself is _____ .

I am CEO of _____ .

And I won't stop trying until I _____ .

GO FOR IT

When you realize you're being hard on yourself, change your playlist. Remember, you're in control of how you think, how you feel, and what you do! If you don't like the song you're playing in your head, hit the "Next" button.

Journal
YOUR BRIGHT IDEAS

What's a problem or doubt that is stuck on a loop in your head? How can you change your attitude toward it?

Don't Let Your Problems Become Louder than Your Progress.

CHAPTER TWENTY-ONE

Run a Relay

O kay, my friend, before we end this journey together, I need you to know just how much your story and your ideas matter. Not just today, not just tomorrow, not just in *your* lifetime but across many future lifetimes to come. People you will never get the chance to meet could be influenced by *your* ideas and actions.

There are multiple people who have greatly influenced me but I never got the chance to meet, like Ruth Bader Ginsburg (RBG). She was a Supreme Court justice who spent her whole life fighting for women's equality. Here are some of the important things she did:

- She cofounded the first law journal on women's rights.
- She fought for Title IX (gender equality in higher-education funding).
- She helped pass a law that says employees cannot be discriminated against because of their gender.
- She helped pass another law that says state-funded schools must admit women.
- And she helped pass another law that say juries must include women.

Because of RBG, I was able to attend a state school where I could get an education that eventually helped me start my own business. Because of her, I and other women were also able to apply for business loans (loans and credit cards used to be available only to men!), and so much more.

In fact, I can see how RBG's life had an impact on my own family. My mom's mom (Grandma Joan) always wanted to work at a meaningful job at an office. But she had three kids before she was twenty-five years old, which was common in the 1960s. Many women had kids and stayed at home while the men worked.

One day, Grandma Joan got a babysitter and secretly took a train into Manhattan. She got off the train and went to the offices of *Publishers Weekly* magazine, which had advertised an open secretary position. She went in, applied for the job, and didn't get it.

She called them a few days later and said, "Hey, if it doesn't work out with the person you hired, call me."

One week later they called her, and the job was hers!

Grandma Joan started as a secretary at *Publishers Weekly* and worked her way up to become the vice president of distribution. Many times, she was the only woman in the boardroom.

Now here's the *crazy* part.

Forty years later, I published my first book called *Chasing the Bright Side. Publishers Weekly* gave it a starred review, and I went to their offices in Manhattan to be interviewed for a press feature.

My grandma told me the name of the man who hired her as a secretary all those years ago, and believe it or not, he was still with the company.

I found his office, wrote him a letter that thanked him for hiring my grandma in 1965, and left the letter on his desk along with a copy of my book. He wrote back and said that hiring Joan was the best decision he ever made! Talk about a full-circle moment.

RBG paved so many roads that were closed for women before, especially improving the workplace for women. Those workplace improvements helped my grandma have a career in a male-dominated world. And watching her do that inspired me to go for it too.

So here's the thing: true success is not about how far you can reach; it's about how far you're helping others reach.

And that might mean the impact of what you do spreads far beyond your lifetime. You might invent something that people still use one hundred years from now. Or you might write a book that's used in your great-great-great grandkids' schools.

One of the most touching letters I have ever received is from a student who said she hung a picture of the two of us (which she took after I spoke at her school) on her bedroom wall. When someone asks, "Who's that in the picture with you?" she replies, "That's the girl who changed my life."

Can you imagine having that kind of impact on someone? Years from now someone could say to you, "Because of *you*, I was able to _____ _____."

Have you ever seen a relay race before? It's where you run a race as a team. One person starts and they run with a baton, then once they finish their leg of the race, they pass the baton to the next runner, and so on.

In a regular race, you run as fast as possible so you can cross the finish line, beat the other runners, and get your trophy. But if you're a runner in a relay race, your goal is to run as hard and fast as possible to put the *next* runner in a good position.

I want you to think about this:

YOUR LIFE IS NOT A RACE TO WIN; IT'S A RELAY TO PARTICIPATE IN.

If you treat your life as a single finish line that you need to cross, then nothing will ever be good enough, because running a solo race is about beating all the other participants, rather than making progress for your team. There will always be people faster and slower than you, and how you compare to them doesn't define who you are. If you're only running for your own finish line, you'll exhaust yourself, and honestly, it's lonely running solo.

> Pass the baton to future generations.

But if you treat your life as a moment in time to *advance* something and then pass the baton to future generations, that's something worth running for. If you're running a relay to help minimize trash and waste to help the environment, that's an impact that will be felt long after you're gone. If you're running a relay to help people feel happy through music, your songs could be listened to for hundreds of years!

I hope my life advances business opportunities for women. I hope women watch my story and think, *If she can do it, I can do it!*

If she can start her business while she's in school, SO CAN I.

If she can bounce back from a failure, **SO CAN I.**

If she can hit millions of dollars in sales, **SO CAN I.**

If she can use her business to give back, **SO CAN I.**

If she can tell her story on stages, **SO CAN I.**

If she can have a dream and do it, SO CAN I.

No matter how much money I make or how many awards I get, I

know my success is about what I've done for others more than about what I've done for myself.

My success is making progress for the future, not what I earn in the present. What if *you* defined success like that too?

Let's end our journey together with The Purpose Test. I'm not a great test taker, but this is one test I like! This will help you figure out if the bright idea you're currently pursuing is truly meaningful to you.

The Purpose Test

1. What business idea, big dream, or world-changing goal are you chasing?

_____

_____

_____

2. Why are you doing it?

_____

_____

_____

3. What does it mean *to you* for this idea or dream to be successful?

_____

_____

_____

Now, here's the kicker. If you reached the level of success you listed under question 3 but nobody knew you were the one who had achieved it, would you chase after that dream anyway? For example, if you dreamed of giving every school a wheelchair access ramp so the front doors were accessible for all kids—but no one knew that *you* were the founder of this idea—would you still do it?

Or imagine you had an idea to knit warm and cozy hats, and for each one you sold, you donated one to a homeless shelter. If no one knew that you were the founder of this business, would you still do it?

Circle: YES/NO

If you circled yes, then **CONGRATS**! You've found a goal that is meaningful to you and gives you purpose.

If you circled no, then let's go back to the drawing board and find an idea that will make you happy even without the fame that may come with success.

So why does this test matter? Because it's so easy to do things based on how popular it is. What will people say? How many likes did I get on social media? Did I get a highlight in my local paper? Will I get an award at school?

I want you to focus on pursuing ideas not based on how they look on the *outside* to *others* but based on how they feel on the *inside* to *you*.

And our gut has a great way of telling us what's meaningful and what isn't.

The Purpose Test doesn't just show you if your idea will be meaningful *to you*; it can show how an idea can change *the world*.

Remember, your life is not a race to be won but a relay to participate in. And if life's a relay, then . . .

- Do everything at your own pace. Try not to compare your stride to someone else's!
- Take care of your teammates because we're all in this together.
- Aim for progress instead of perfection. It's not about getting it right all the time; it's about moving forward.
- Be kind to others in their race. We're all running for different things, so let's support each other!
- Get back up when you fall. You'll make mistakes, but that's a normal part of the process.
- Run in the direction of your North Star and always remind yourself what you're running for.

Now go create your bright ideas!

GO FOR IT

Do The Purpose Test for all your big ideas. Which of your ideas are worth going for even without the recognition? Once you find that answer, start creating those ideas!

Journal
YOUR BRIGHT IDEAS

What is a cause, mission, or purpose that you want to contribute to? What kind of impact do you want to have in your lifetime?

Create Your Own Business Plan

Your name: _____

Business Plan for _____

(Fill in your business name here.)

Mission Statement

A mission statement is a one-sentence summary of why your company exists. You want someone to read your mission statement and say, "Oh! I totally understand what they do and why they do it. I can't wait to be a customer!"

A mission statement is also helpful for you as the founder. It will help guide your decision making. You can always ask yourself, "Is this opportunity serving my mission statement?" You can guide your company and make decisions based on if something will serve your mission.

1. Who are you helping (your intended customer)?

2. What problem do you see in the world (your itch)?

3. How is your business going to help that problem (your scratch)? How will a customer's life be better *after* they buy your product?

4. What kind of product are you going to sell to solve the problem?

Your mission statement is:

We help

(Fill in your answer to #1 here.)

overcome

(Fill in your answer to #2 here.)

so they can

(Fill in your answer to #3 here.)

by creating

(Fill in your answer to #4 here.)

Where do you want to sell your products (online, in stores, or both)?

Who is your target customer? Who could benefit the most from using your products?

How do you want to market to your target customers? How will they discover you?

How much will it cost to make each product? (Figuring out an estimate will be helpful. It doesn't have to be exact.) This is called your *COGS* (cost of goods sold).

Then, how much do you want to sell it for? This is called the *MSRP* (manufacturer's suggested retail price)—so fancy!

What is your profit?

Helpful Tip: Take your MSRP and subtract your COGS. For example, a bracelet-making business spends $10 for the beads, string, and shipping, and then sells each bracelet on its website for $30.

$30 (MSRP) – $10 (COGS) = a profit margin of $20

What are your financial goals for your business?

What are your nonmonetary impact goals for your business? In other words, how do you want your business to help people and the world?

A month from now, what would you like to have done?

Six months from now, what would you like to have done?

A year from now, what would you like to have done?

Notes

Letter from jess

1. Peter Economy, "This Is the Way You Need to Write Down Your Goals for Faster Success," Inc., February 28, 2018, https://www.inc.com/peter-economy /this-is-way-you-need-to-write-down-your-goals-for-faster-success.html.

Chapter Eight: Make It Matter

1. Zee, "It Doesn't Take 10,000 Hours to Learn a New Skill. It Takes 20. And Here's How . . .," TNW, October 24, 2013, https://thenextweb.com/news /doesnt-take-10000-hours-learn-skill-takes-20-heres-now.

Chapter Twelve: Make a Mess

1. Robby Berman, "New Study Suggests We Have 6,200 Thoughts Every Day," Big Think, July 16, 2020, https://bigthink.com/neuropsych/how-many -thoughts-per-day/.

Chapter Seventeen: Show Up

1. Dr. John Muzhuthettu, "The Amazing Psychology of Luck," *The Daily Brunch*, February 18, 2018, https://thedailybrunch.com/2018/02/18/the -amazing-psychology-of-luck/.

Chapter Eighteen: Don't Wait for Instant Success

1. Sebastian Kipman, "15 Highly Successful People Who Failed Before Succeeding," Lifehack, March 16, 2022, https://www.lifehack.org/articles /productivity/15-highly-successful-people-who-failed-their-way-success.html.

Chapter Twenty: Pick Your Song

1. Walter A. Brown, "Expectation, the Placebo Effect and the Response to Treatment," *Rhode Island Medical Journal*, May 2015, http://www.rimed.org /rimedicaljournal/2015/05/2015-05-19-cont-brown.pdf.

About the Author

Jess Ekstrom began her entrepreneurial journey as a kid selling her toys on eBay. Today, Jess is a prominent speaker, a serial social entrepreneur, and the founder of Headbands of Hope, Mic Drop Workshop, and Prompted.io. Headbands of Hope has been featured on *TODAY*, *Good Morning America*, QVC, and *The View* and has been worn by celebrities like Kelsea Ballerini and Khloé Kardashian. More importantly, Headbands of Hope has donated over one million headbands, reaching every single children's hospital in America and twenty-two countries. She's the author of *Chasing the Bright Side* and a big fan of breakfast burritos. Jess and her husband, Jake, and their seventy-pound dog, Ollie, live in Raleigh, North Carolina.

The bright idea that started it all...

HEADBANDS
of hope

For every headband sold, one is donated to a child with an illness.

Get 20% off your first order with the code **BRIGHT** at www.headbandsofhope.com.